HISTORY

— OF —

TAOS

Historia de Taos

NM

HISTORY

— OF —

TAOS

Historia de Taos

F. R. BOB ROMERO

ISBN: 978-0-692-40021-0

Design/Layout: Studio Karina, LLC
Lesley Cox, Ana Karina Armijo, Contessa Trujillo
Taos, New Mexico

Cover Illustration: Donald Ward
Editing: Contessa Trujillo
Type is set in Paliard and Aleo

To Alice, my wife, who inspired me
to see this book come to fruition.

Foreword

History of Taos (*Historia De Taos*) tells the fascinating story of Taos. This 400 year commemorative edition about the founding of Taos chronicles the various topics and events that make up the rich, long, and diverse history of Taos, New Mexico. The 25 sub-topics include the prominent historical figures of Taos such as Po'pay, Padre Martinez, and Kit Carson as well as the major historical sites and landmarks like The Taos Pueblo, La Hacienda de los Martinez, and the historic churches of Taos. The entire history of Taos including the pre-history is outlined chronologically and concisely in a timeline that is divided into the four time-periods of Taos. An overview of History of Taos is presented in Spanish in the epic poem entitled "*Yo Soy Taoseno*."

Besides serving to help commemorate 400 years of Taos history, the objective of this book is to fill the need for a short book about the history of Taos that is concise, condensed, and that is written for the present. In this book the past is not simply the past, it is an integral part of the present and also is a tool to help plan for the future. This profile of Taos history not only presents the events, historical figures, historical landmarks and the institutions of Taos, but it also is a search for the characteristics that gives Taos its true identity.

Introduction

The 400 year celebration of the history of Taos served as the inspiration for the completion of this pocket book history of Taos. The year 2015 marks the "*Cuarto Centenario*" or the 400th anniversary of the year that Taos became Taos. The Taos Pueblo had existed for some 200-300 years before 1615, but it had been known by at least seven other names that include Yuraba, Uraba, Braba, San Miguel, Tu-o-ta, Tayberon, and Valledolid. The name Taos as it is known today, however, is first found in the journals that document the Don Juan de Oñate colonization of New Mexico in 1598, and by 1615 the Taos Pueblo was officially declared a village or villa by the Spanish Colonial Government and thus became known as El Pueblo de Taos or Taos Pueblo.

The completion of this short history of Taos postmarks a personal milestone for the author, F.R. Bob Romero, since he collaborated with Robin Collier and Mike Tilly to produce a radio program through Cultural Energy that aired on KRZA. The radio program called "*Historia De Taos*" entailed more than twenty brief broadcasts that focused on the history of Taos. More recently he worked with Mr. Glen Pike to reproduce this same program in a video format. The 25 sub-topics contained in the book thus represent the third rendition or refinement as the 25 chapters that survey the History of Taos.

Acknowledgements

I want to express sincere thanks to numerous individuals that helped me in some capacity to complete this short History of Taos. First and foremost I want to thank my wife, Alice and good friend Amos Martinez who regularly and routinely asked "How is the manuscript on the History of Taos coming?" I also want to thank my son Carlos who proof read the text and provided technical and legal support for the project.

Special thanks also go to Donald Ward who created the sketch for the book cover, and Ana Karina Armijo who so diligently served as graphic artist and Contessa Trujillo for editing of the book. Finally, I want to thank Corina A. Santistevan who has been my mentor and has always encouraged me in my pursuit of preserving the past and specifically in researching, reading, and writing the history of Taos.

Table of Contents

Taos History Timeline

Historia De Taos Línea De Tiempo

PRE-HISTORY
Time Immemorial - 1540 A.D.

1000 A.D.
Splinter groups of Anasazi Indians started establishing permanent settlement in the Taos Valley living in pit houses.

| 1000 A.D. | 1350 |

1350 A.D.
Taos Pueblo was constructed after residents of Pot Creek Pueblo abandoned Pot Creek between 1320-1350 and moved to Taos to build multi-storied structures. The people survived by planting corn, beans, and squash and by hunting small game.

SPANISH EXPLORATION & COLONIAL PERIOD
1540 - 1821 A.D.

1540 A.D.
Captain Hernando De Alvarado led a contingent of the Coronado Expedition into Taos in 1540. They were the first Europeans on record to see Taos.

1680 A.D.
The Pueblo Revolt of 1680, led by Po'pay, forced the Spanish settlers out of New Mexico. In Taos more than 70 Spaniards were killed including 2 Franciscan Priests.

| 1540 | 1598 | 1680 | 1696 |

1598 A.D.
Don Juan De Onate colonized New Mexico for the Spanish Empire, and he is placed in Taos on July 14, 1598.

1696 A.D.
Don Diego De Vargas completed the Re-Conquest of New Mexico when he arrived in Taos, and persuaded Taos Pueblo Indians to drop their arms and return to the Pueblo.

1723 A.D.
This is the first recorded date of a Taos Trade Fair although similar trading events of the Native Americans preceded the Taos Trade Fair that continued into the 1800s when the Mountain Men arrived and joined in.

1723   1815

1815 A.D.
The Ranchos San Francisco De Asis Church is completed when the alter screen retablos were installed and mass is celebrated. The Ranchos Church is the most photographed and painted church in New Mexico and one of the most recognized in the country.

MEXICAN PERIOD
1821 - 1846 A.D.

1821 A.D.
Taos became part of
the Republic of Mexico
after an II year war for
Independence initiated by
Father Miguel Hidalgo.

1822 A.D.
Padre Martinez returned
to New Mexico after being
ordained as a secular priest in
Mexico during the Mexican
struggle for independence.

1821 1822   1826   1832

1826 A.D.
The Hacienda Martinez was at
its peak of development and
activity after being founded by
Severino Martinez in 1804.

1832 A.D.
Padre Martinez organized the
Penitentes into the Moradas
to protect the privacy of the
rituals of penance, faith, and
devotion.

1837 A.D.
Taoseños participated in the Revolt of 1837 against the Mexican Government over taxes and incompetence and corruption in the government. Jose Gonzales, a mixed-blood Taoseño from Ranchos de Taos, was selected interim governor of New Mexico for 6 months before he was captured and executed by Manuel Armijo who repressed the Revolt.

1837   1846

1846 A.D.
Stephen Watts Kearny marched into New Mexico with the "Army of the West" and occupied New Mexico. United States sovereignty became official 2 years later when the Treaty of Guadalupe Hidalgo was signed in 1848 at the conclusion of the Mexican American War.

UNITED STATES SOVEREIGNTY
1846 - Present

1847 A.D.
In the Taos Revolt/Resistance of 1847 Governor Charles Bent, the first American Governor of New Mexico, was murdered in Taos on January 19, 1847 after an alliance of Pueblo Indians and Hispano firebrand nationalists attacked the Americans.

1898 A.D.
Artists Ernest Blumenschein and Bert Phillips arrived in Taos when their wagon wheel broke on a sketching trip from Denver to Mexico.

1847   1861   1898 1915

1861 A.D.
Kit Carson and Captain Smith Simpson and others took it upon themselves to guard the U.S. flag around the clock on the Taos Plaza when it was torn down by some Confederate sympathizers.

1915 A.D.
Taos Society of Artists is formed which led to Taos becoming a world renowned artist colony.

1965 A.D.
The Rio Grande George Bridge is completed. This milestone opened Taos to the North and to the West.

1956	1965	1967

1967 A.D.
The New Buffalo Commune was founded in Arroyo Hondo, and the Hippie Invasion of Taos occurred in the late 1960s.

1956 A.D.
Taos Ski Valley (TSV) was started by Ernie and Rhoda Blake. This began Taos' transformation into a recreational and resort destination.

I

The Founding of Taos

La Fundación De Taos

The time or specific date that a community like Taos is founded is usually determined by the year that people first settled on a location and began to build permanent structures. Jamestown, Virginia and Santa Fe, New Mexico are classic examples of this notion, but nothing with Taos, NM, especially its founding, is quite so simple. The founding date of Taos is not definitive since the earliest indigenous founding dates are ambiguous and Taos may in fact have both an indigenous origination and a separate and important European founding date.

In any case, we can begin to shed light as to when Taos was settled by looking back chronologically from recent events. The Town of Taos was recently incorporated as a municipality in 1934[1]. Another older important date that is also commonly noted by historians is 1796 when the Don Fernando de Taos Land Grant was ceded to the people of Taos, and the Town of Taos Plaza had its origins at that time. The Ranchos de Taos Plaza had already been under construction for some years earlier before 1776, but the beginning of these two important plazas cannot accurately be considered to be the founding date or the beginning of Taos either, because so much happened earlier in the Taos Valley.[2]

A strong case can be made for a European settlement date between 1610 and 1619, or specifically 1615, a date that is inscribed on a sign on the Taos Plaza. This is the time when, San Jeronimo, the first Catholic Church was being constructed at the Taos Pueblo,

Taos Pueblo was proclaimed a Village by the Spanish government and the Spanish Colonists began to settle in the Taos Valley.[3] This then makes Taos arguably the fourth oldest community in the United States from the European point of view. In chronological order, St. Augustine FL (1565) is the oldest, Jamestown, VA (1607) is the oldest British colony, Santa Fe, NM (1610) is the third oldest community in the country and Taos, NM (1615) is the fourth oldest inhabited European community in the U.S.[4]

Moreover, in the discussion on the founding of Taos we must acknowledge dates such as 1598 when Don Juan de Onate colonized New Mexico and actually began using the Taos name as we know it today, instead of the Indian name or word from which Taos was probably derived. In addition we also need to take note of 1540 and 1541 when Hernando de Alvarado and Velasco de Barrionuevo became the first Europeans to visit Taos. These are also important dates although they should not be considered founding dates for Taos either since these Spanish explorers visited but did not build physical structures or make permanent settlement in Taos.

Finally, considering the Native American perspective which for many people is the most significant, the founding date or the early settlement of Taos may not be a linear or a chronological number. Instead it is more about time in space or place or a creationist outlook without a strict focus as to sequence or specific dates. The onset of the construction of the structures at the Taos Pueblo around 1350 A.D. and the earlier settlement of the Taos Tiwa People in the Taos Valley around 1000 A.D. are the earliest settlements and are also the indigenous founding dates of Taos Pueblo.[5] These events then makes Taos Pueblo one of the oldest continuously inhabited communities in North America and the oldest town in the present day United States.

So in essence when Taos was founded is relative and depends on multiple perspectives. Perhaps the most plausible explanation is that Taos has both an important indigenous origination and a distinctive and relevant European founding that is commemorated in this "Cuarto Centenario" edition. In any case the mystique of the genesis of Taos, since it is so old, is a topic that continues to fascinate and to mystify people to the present day.

Footnotes

1. Town of Taos, Vision 2020 Master Plan, Mayor Fred Peralta and Town of Taos Council, Adopted February 1999, p. 24 Ibid., p. 21
2. Ibid., p. 20 GD120 Justicia Eclesiastica, vol. 101, f. 328-338. NUEVO MEXICO, 1831. Sobre conceder parroco propio a la villa de San Geronimo de Taos, del territorio de Santa Fe. Archivos General de la Nacion (Archives Of Mexico City)
3. Ibid., p. 20 GD127 Gobernacion: Sin Seccion, caja 116, exp. 100, fs. 1-4. Ano: s/f Sobre que se le concede al territorio de Taos el character de Villa. Archivos General de la Nacion (Achives of Mexico City)
4. Ibid., p.20
5. Corina A. Santistevan and Julia Moore, eds., Taos a topical History, (Santa Fe: Museum of New Mexico Press, Publishers, 2013, pp. 14, 138

2

The Four Time-periods of Taos History

Los Cuatro Pediodos
De La Historia De Taos

T he pre-history or Pueblo Era (time immemorial–1540), is the first of the four time-periods of Taos History. This is the time in the past that is not recorded or that as far as is known is not part of the historical record. Scholars have concluded from the study of artifacts and the body of knowledge produced by anthropologists and archeologists that Big Game Hunters were in New Mexico and probably passed through the Taos Valley some 9000-10000 years ago in pursuit of migratory animals that they hunted for their livelihood.[1] More recent Indigenous People known to archeologists as the "Anasazi" arrived in New Mexico much later, around 2000 years ago or around the time of Christ and then migrated into the Taos Valley about 1000 years later. The first people in Taos Valley lived in pit houses and later at Cornfield Pueblo. People also lived at the Llano Quemado Pueblo and the large Pot Creek Pueblo which was built in the 1200s. The existing Taos Pueblo was constructed in the 14th century around 1350 A.D., and is the only one of these pre-historic structures still standing.[2] These four major sites along with other archeological sites are all part of the pre-history of Taos.

The written history of Taos begins in 1540 with the arrival of the Spanish Conquistadors as part of the Coronado Expedition that explored into the Taos Valley.[3] Hernando de Alvarado is on the record as the first European in Taos, although the permanent colonization of Nuevo Mexico and Taos by Don

Juan de Onate occurred in 1598. The era of Spanish presence in Taos continued through the 1600s, with the exception of the years following the Pueblo Revolt of 1680. Since the continuity of the European settlement was severed, some historians have questioned the significance of the early 1600s settlement. However, the Spanish Re-conquest was completed by Don Diego De Vargas in 1696, and Spanish colonists returned permanently to the Taos Valley.

The settlers that arrived in the 18th century oversaw the growth of a self-sufficient agrarian based society built upon the development of the acequias, land grants, haciendas and, ranchitos that were occupied and worked by the large extended pioneer families. These families were a mixture of Spanish and Native Americans and the descendants of these two bloodlines continued to mix since first contact between the Spanish and Native Americans. The blended Nuevo Mexicano settlers were hard-working and God-fearing families seeking to survive in an arid and inhospitable frontier environment that was made even more dangerous by the unrelenting nomadic and plains Indian raids in the 1700s into the Taos Valley. The Spanish colonists in Taos survived with the help of the mission churches and hospitality of the people of Taos Pueblo and they even began to thrive, but by the early 1800s the sunset of Spanish Rule was on the horizon and the next time-period of Taos History was imminent.

With the United State purchase of the Louisiana Territory in 1803 the number of trappers and traders from the Eastern United States began as a trickle and then the floodgates of immigrants from American Colonies opened widely with Mexican Independence in 1821. The opening of the Santa Fe Trail in 1821 happened simultaneously with the onset of the Mexican Period, and the short time-period of Mexican Rule from 1821-1846 was a transitional era that laid the groundwork for American occupation of New Mexico. This was the onset of what was essentially an economic conquest of New Mexico by the U.S.

However, the Mexican Period is a remarkable and interesting time-period in Taos marked by the spirited activities of the newly arrived mountain men such as Kit Carson, the resurgence and reorganization of the Hermanos Penitentes under the spiritual guidance of Padre Martinez, and the passionate pursuits of Padre Martinez in education, religion, government, and publishing. In the Revolt of 1837 the People of Northern New Mexico rebelled against the Mexican Government, and almost followed in the footsteps of their neighboring state of Texas in a notable event that resembled Texas' independence from Mexico one year earlier in 1836. Jose Gonzales from Ranchos de Taos was installed as governor of New Mexico for six months before he was captured and executed. The rebellion was then cut short and New Mexico and Taos remained under Mexican Rule until

1846 when Stephen Watts Kearny occupied New Mexico without firing a shot. This began the fourth time-period of Taos history now known as United States Sovereignty. The Taos Revolt/Resistance of 1847 against American occupation was planned and executed in Taos. It was a major event in New Mexico history because of the death of Governor Bent, but it also was short-lived and did not reverse American occupation.

The time-period of United States Sovereignty has been noted for the introduction of the cash economy and free-enterprise system, as well as a democratic system of government that promotes constitutional liberties and civil rights. Much economic development and modernization such as schools, roads, hospitals, state and local government, and modern conveniences of telecommunications and public utilities has happened under American Sovereignty. The time-period of United Sovereignty in Taos is now more than one-and-half century in duration and has been characterized by dramatic change and progress in the Taos area. Taosenos are full blown, loyal, and patriotic Americans but still are the product of their past and proudly retain their traditional cultural heritage from the previous time-periods.

In summation, the four historical time-periods of Taos are the Pre-history period that includes the early Taos Pueblo era (Time immemorial to 1540), the beginning of recorded history and the Spanish Exploration and Colonial Period from 1540-1821, the Mexican Period from 1821-1846, and American Sovereignty from 1846-present.

Footnotes

1. Town of Taos, Vision 2020 Master Plan, Mayor Fred Peralta and Town of Taos council, adopted February 1999, p. 19
2. Corina A Santistevan and Julia Moore eds., Taos A Topical History, (Santa Fe: Museum of New Mexico Press, Publishers, 2013), pp 36-39
3. George P. Hammond and Agapito Rey, eds. Narrative Of The Coronado Expedition 1540-1542, (Albuquerque, 1940), pp. 288-289
   Also refer to New Mexico Historical Review XLI: 1966, Myra Ellen Jenkins: Taos Pueblo, pp. 86, 87

3

Origins of the Taos Name

El Origin Del Nombre De Taos

The Taos name is not found in the Spanish historical accounts until the Juan de Onate Colonization of New Mexico in 1598. Prior to this date the recorded accounts of the area we now know as the Taos Valley, Town of Taos, and Taos Pueblo had other names or designations. For example in the Coronado Journals and old maps of the area Taos was identified at different times as Braba, Uraba, Yuraba, Tayberon, and Valledolid.[1]

Beginning with the Onate Colonization Journals that documented the Onate Colonization, we see the name of Taos scripted for the first time, which then morphed into Don Fernando de Taos in honor of Don Fernando Duran y Chavez, one of the first Spanish settlers in the Taos Valley in the early 1600s.[2] The name Don Fernando de Taos then received another boost in 1796 when Fernando Chacon, the Governor of New Mexico ceded the Don Fernando de Taos Land Grant to citizens of Taos. Later in the middle 1800s the village of Taos was also referred to as Don Fernandez de Taos and San Fernandez de Taos. But these longer variations of the name were finally abbreviated to just Taos and thus Taos is what has survived to the present day although sometimes in different American or English variations such a Taosi or Tay-os.

Some writers have attributed the Taos name to Tao (The Way) or Taoism, the Chinese religion and philosophy that advocates simplicity and selflessness.[3] Mystically and esoterically this idea does have a certain kind of sentimental or spiritual appeal, but there is no known documented historical connection that directly links Tao and Taos. According to John J. Bodine, an anthropologist who worked at the Taos Pueblo in the 1970s, "Taos is most definitely not related to Chinese."[4]

Contemporary historians and writers have also speculated about the origin of the Taos name as having being derived from the Indian word Tu-o-ta perhaps meaning "Red Willow" or "People of Red Willow". In essence, the conjecture is that Taos is derived from an Indian word presumably one that begins with a T and sounds like Taos, perhaps even Tua-Tah which may mean "down at the village". However, in speaking with some people from Taos Pueblo they do not readily confirm this and quite often and quite adamantly state that Taos is not an Indian word or a Tiwa term and that there is no obvious word in the Tiwa language that refers to Red Willow. In addition, Taos is not a Spanish word or an Arabic or Latin term from which many words in the Spanish language are derived.

So what is the origin of the Taos name? It is safe to say that the mystery of the origins of the Taos name, similarly to the mystery of the founding date of Taos, are part of its enduring mystique. The name of Taos did originate historically at the time of the Onate Colonization as this is part of the historical record. The word is probably the Hispanicized or pluralized version of an Indian word that may or may not refer to Red Willow place or people, or the village. Without question it has been embraced by all Taosenos that live in Taos and who love Taos. Taos is more than a reference to a Town or County or Indian Pueblo, Art Colony, or Ski Resort. Taos also has connotations of an attitude or state of mind that entails longevity, tenacity, resiliency, vitality, and even eccentricity. Or, as the popular bumper sticker about

Taos Ski Valley states, perhaps Taos is a four letter word that means steep.

Footnotes

1. Myra Ellen Jenkins, "Taos Pueblo and Its Neighbors," New Mexico Historical Review 41:2 1966, pp. 86,87 GD127Gobernacion: Sin Seccion, caja 99, exp. 1, fs. 40. Ano: S/F. *Se nombra Villa a Taos, Nuevo Mexico. Archivos
General de la Nacion (Archives of Mexico City).
2. George P. Hammond and Agapito Rey, eds. Don Juan de Onate: Colonizer of New Mexico, 1595-1598, (Albuquerque: University of New Mexico Press, 1953, p. 321, In this account the name of Taos as it is known today is first recorded, and it is also stated that it "had also been called Tayberon and others."
3. Blanche C. Grant, When Old Trails Were New,The Story of Taos, (Glorietta: The Rio Grande Press), 1983, p. 3
4. John J. Bodine, Taos Pueblo: A Walk Through Time, (Santa Fe, The Lightning Tree, Jene Lyon Publisher, 1977), p. 39

4

The Geologic Past Of The Taos Valley

La Geologia Y Topografia De Taos

Two of the most spectacular views in the Taos Valley are the northwestern and southern advances into Taos. Both the Taos Valley Overlook and the Rio Grande Gorge Bridge entrances tell a big part of the story of the geologic past of the mountain ringed Valley of Taos. Geologically, Taos Valley has impressive diversity in terms of the topography, flora and fauna, the landforms, and landscapes and has some of the most diverse, dynamic and breathtaking views in the world.[1]

The views as seen from the south are stunning. At first, a person that drives north out of the Horseshoe on State Road 68 is faced with the spectacular views of the meandering Rio Grande Gorge. Immediately after that view, looking northeast one is confronted with the sights of the majestic and sacred Taos Mountain and the Sangre de Cristo Range that are part of the uplift of the earth's crust that created the Southern Rocky Mountains. Behind the Taos Mountain is Mount Wheeler, the highest point in New Mexico at 13,161 feet that is part of the Columbine–Hondo Wilderness. Mount Wheeler and other peaks were shaped by glaciers during the last ice age as were Blue Lake and Williams Lake.

In striking contrast to the higher mountain peaks to the east, the Tres Orejas peaks to the west, and Ute Mountain to the north are visible examples of the numerous dormant cinder or dome cones. These landforms are evidence of an active and transformative geological history on the Taos Plateau also known as the Taos Mesa. An even more distant view to the Northwest is the San Antonio Mountain, a large extinct dome volcano, that is the "largest free standing mountain in the country." To the South you can see the Jicarita Peak in the distance near Penasco, and the surrounding prong or the Picuris Range that encircles the Taos Valley to the south. The volcanic and uplifted mountain ranges together surround the entire valley that includes the dry and barren areas west of the Rio Grande Gorge near Carson and the agrarian well watered eastern part of the Valley.

Over time, geologically and at a glacial pace the Taos Valley landscape has changed remarkably from a placid setting with tropical seas with white sand beaches, to sand dunned deserts, to lush forests, and massive mountains.[2] Taos Valley is blessed in the present day to have six rivers that flow out of the surrounding mountains and five of these streams come together into a confluence at

Los Cordovas where they empty into the Rio Pueblo which then flows into the Rio Grande. The acequias (ditches) that were built in past centuries in the Taos Valley for irrigation purposes flow serenely in the spring and summer from these tributaries.

The Rio Grande Rift is a geologic feature that is about 30 million years old, 6 miles deep and 20 miles wide and can be traced along Highway 522 from Questa towards Taos. The rift was filled in over the centuries by vast amounts of gravel, lava, and ash. This fault line will not make any sudden or dramatic changes to the landscape any time soon, but it is a powerful natural presence, nonetheless.[3] In its evolution, the Rio Grande found the rift trough and followed it, cutting a deep imposing gorge over the millennia. So it was not a sudden cataclysmic event that formed the gorge as some have believed, but instead a slow process of 100,000 years of water running through volcanic rock.[4] The lava layers that are visible from the high bridge spanning the gorge west of Taos are broken into columns formed by the distinctive way in which the volcanic material settled and cooled.

The Rio Grande Gorge Bridge has become one of the most popular landmarks around Taos. The Gorge Bridge, once known as "the bridge to nowhere" due to lack of funding when it was being built, was dedicated on September 10, 1965 in honor of Governor Jack M. Campbell who worked to secure funding to see the bridge come to fruition.[5] The completed U.S. 64 Road opened up Taos Valley for commerce and access to the west and north and passes through some spectacular scenery in northern New Mexico.

In summary, the Rio Grande Gorge Bridge is a physical structure made by man out of steel beams, and is utilitarian in the way it is utilized for travel across the gorge. In addition the bridge and the gorge provide an awesome view of the diverse natural environment that along with the surrounding mountains gave Taos Valley its historic isolation. The Rio Grande Rift is mysterious because it is not visible to the naked eye but is a deep geologic fault line or fissure that is also partly responsible for the natural beauty that we see around us today, and is part of the physical diversity and geological past of Taos Valley. The Rio Grande Gorge and the surrounding Taos Plateau and San Antonio and Ute Mountains are part of the Rio Grande del Norte National Monument that was proclaimed by President Barrack Obama on March 25, 2013. The geological and natural features surrounding Taos give some credence to the grand claim by some that Taos is a power center of the universe.

Footnotes

1. Corina A. Santistevan and Julia Moore, eds., Taos A Topical History (Santa Fe: Museum of New Mexico Press, Publishers, 2013), p.19
2. Ibid. p. 20
3. Ibid. p. 24
4. Ibid. p. 27
5. The Taos News, September 1-7, 2011, My Turn, "Why Don't They Bridge It?" John Himes, p. A7

5

The Taos Pueblo
El Pueblo De Taos

The Taos Pueblo is the oldest town in America, the oldest continuously inhabited residence in the United States, and the most popular historical landmark and tourist attraction in Taos. Thousands of people visit this iconic Indian village every year. The Taos pueblo is recognized as a World Heritage Site and is on the Registry of National Historic Places. The current name of Taos Pueblo is not found in the historical record until after Spanish colonization in 1598, but the Tiwa speaking community had existed for 200-300 years earlier, although under other names.

We do not know precisely how old the site of the Taos Pueblo settlement is because we do not have indisputable archeological evidence. Until a 1961 excavation by archeologists, occupation of this large pueblo had been but a guess.[1] Archeologists now conjecture that the Pueblo dates to about 1350 A.D. Historians do not know from a strictly historical perspective when the current structures were constructed either because the date was probably not documented. If it was documented the date is a closely guarded secret known only within the Taos Pueblo walls and kiva clans. We do know from the study of archeologists that there was once also a "Cornfield Pueblo" established sometime after clan groups of different languages and of several origins had settled in the Taos Valley initially around 1000 A.D.[2]

John J. Bodine an anthropologist placed the construction of the Taos Pueblo at 1450 A.D., and it is entirely possible that the building of the entire Pueblo took 100 years and thus was then completed around 1450 A.D. We do know definitively that the Pueblo as it stands today was in existence in 1540 A.D. when the Spanish Conquistadors first arrived in the Taos Valley because this was written into the Spanish journals and is well documented.[3]

The Taos Pueblo today is located approximately two miles north of the present day Town of Taos on the Taos Pueblo Land Grant ceded by the Spanish Government in the 1600s and patented by the U.S. government in 1864.[4] The Taos Tiwa People trace their spiritual origins and their life source to the sacred Blue Lake that was returned by the United States government to the ownership of the Taos Pueblo in 1970. The sacred Blue Lake Ceremony and rituals that take place in late August of each year, in the mountains above the village, symbolize the integrity and unity of the Tribe and are very important to the maintenance of the traditional Taos Pueblo culture and kiva based theo-social system and family structures.

San Geronimo Day, September 30th is another event of great importance to the Taos Pueblo people. Named by the Catholic Church after St. Jerome, the patron saint of the Pueblo, where after four centuries the majority of the people remain Catholic. The celebration was originally a fall trading festival at which neighboring tribes would gather. After Spanish Colonization, San Geronimo (Jeronimo) Day was institutionalized, and today continues with activities that include the morning foot races and the afternoon pole climb. The ceremonial life of the Tribe also includes the Deer Dance, the Buffalo Dance, and the Turtle Dance as well as the dramatic Christmas Eve Procession and the Christmas Day Matachines Dance.[5]

For the Indians of the Taos Pueblo, life has been a continuous struggle against the external forces and people that have routinely migrated into Taos. These invasions and influxes of people included the Nomadic Indians such as the Apaches, Navajo, Utes and Comanches, the Spanish conquistadors and Franciscan missionaries in the 16th century and Spanish settlers of the 1700s, the French trappers and traders in the 1700s, and finally Americans in pursuit of Manifest Destiny in 1846. This was followed by the arrival of the artists in 1898, and "Bohemians" and avant garde intellectuals in the early 1900s and hippies in the late 1960s. The People of Taos Pueblo have miraculously survived all out-side influences and have retained their core essence.

The Taos Pueblo still maintains its tribal sovereignty and its own government and native spirituality based in the oneness of all living things and nature. Some members of the tribe work in Taos, others work for tribal programs and others are employed through the considerable tourism economy of the Tribe, including the Taos Mountain Casino.

The Taos Pueblo is the oldest continually inhabited community in the United States. The Indians of Taos Pueblo remain resilient and fiercely independent of spirit and mind. They continue to speak Tiwa, which is still an unwritten language, and they strive to maintain a balance between their traditional way of life and the modern world.[6]

Footnotes

1. Ceramic Stratigraphy and Tribal History At Taos Pueblo, Florence Hawley Ellis and J.J. Brody, 1964, AM, Antiquity 29 (3): 316-317
2. Ibid. p. 318
3. John J. Bodine, Taos Pueblo: A Walk Through Time, (Santa Fe, The Lightning Tree, Jene Lyon Publisher, 1977), p. 29
4. Corina A. Santistevan and Julia Moore eds., Taos A Topical History, (Santa Fe: Museum of New Mexico History Press, Publishers, 2013), p. 81
5. F.R. Bob Romero and Neil Poese, A Brief History Of Taos, (Taos: Kit Carson Historic Museum, 1992), p. 4 The Patron Saint of the Church at the Taos Pueblo is St. Jerome, but at some point , perhaps after Mexican Independence, the name of the Church became San Geronimo (name of the famous Apache Chief), and contemporary literature on the Church remains San Geromino.
6. Ibid. p. 5

6

Pioneer Trails And Historic Roads Into Taos

Vererdas Y Caminos Antiquos De Taos

D espite being geographically isolated throughout its history, Taos has long been known as a crossroads as Indian trails led into Taos from all four directions, and the trails were perhaps used by pre-historic Big Game Hunters in pursuit of their game.[1] The Kiowa Trail to the north towards Questa was primarily a trail of commerce as the Pueblo Indians traded with the Plains Indians before the Spanish period of exploration. The road to Angel Fire and Cimarron was also known as the Apache

Trail and is now Highway 585 to the East. But Taos because of its geology and terrain was notoriously a difficult place to get to.[2]

The historic trails and roads into Taos from the South are the most intriguing and varied and all the Spanish entradas (entrances) into the Taos Valley approached from the south. The earliest Spanish road that followed Native American trails was the branch of the Camino Real or Royal Road that crossed over from the Espanola area across the Black Mesa and over the Picuris range into Taos Valley crossing by the Ponce de Leon Hot Springs, by the location of the Holy Cross Hospital, and on to the Taos Pueblo. This was the route that was later followed by Juan de Onate in 1598, and Don Diego de Vargas in 1694 and 1696. Another road that was used to travel to Taos during the Spanish Colonial Period also passed through Espanola, Velarde, and Pilar and then climbed in the direction of the Horseshoe. The road then decended into Taos Valley but not on what is now State

Road 68, instead towards Los Cordovas and along Ranchitos Road. It then continued in the proximity of the Hacienda Martinez and towards Taos and the Taos Pueblo.[3]

The third major road into the Taos Valley during the Spanish Era was the Camino del Medio or Middle Road that was established before the time of the first granting of the Cristobal de la Serna Land Grant in 1710 and conveniently served as the western boundary of the Serna Grant. Camino del Medio was in fact the middle road in the Valley at that time and it was a road that extended along the Picuris Ridge all the way and on a straight course directly to Picuris Pueblo as stated by noted trailblazer Charles Hawk who has researched, walked, and written about the roads and historic trails in Taos.[4]

Most of the current roads into Taos were built after American Sovereignty. SR 68 which morphs into Paseo del Pueblo Sur enters from the South as it trails out of the

Horseshoe and swings by the Taos Valley Overlook, then passes through Ranchos de Taos and the Town of Taos. The southern part of the road was built by the United States Military in the canyon along the Rio Grande in the 1880s. The road was not completely paved until the 1950s. The road to Las Vegas, NM or SR 518 was also a Camino Militar (military road) built over the U.S. Hill in the 1860s. U.S. Road 64 from east to west across the Rio Grande Gorge Bridge was not completed until 1965 when state funding was secured to complete the Bridge.

In general, access and travel into Taos is somewhat of a contradiction in that Taos historically has been a crossroads and destination point and at the same time has remained relatively isolated due to its geological barriers and historical circumventions. On the one hand Native Americans regularly and routinely traveled into the Taos Valley to live and to trade, including to the Taos Trade Fairs in the 1700s and early 1800s. The Spaniards arrived in the 1500s and the Frenchmen entered the Valley from the Northeast to trade also at the Taos Fairs in the mid-1700s. American traders and Mountain Men began arriving in the early 1800s, and then entered enmasse when the Santa Fe Trail opened in 1821.

The railroads were built into New Mexico beginning in 1879, and the Chile Line from Colorado reached the Taos Junction south of town, but Taos itself was bypassed by the railroads and the Santa Fe Trail and thus remained isolated in the 1800s as opposed to much of the rest of New Mexico. Taos was again circumvented in the 20th century by the interstate highway system that was routed from Colorado on I-25 through Las Vegas, NM and Santa Fe. The pioneer trails and roads into Taos, however, have been traversed for hundreds of years and include some "of the oldest continuously traveled roads in the country".[5] Some have said that the roads into Taos and in Taos were built not for cars and trucks, but instead for burros and horses. Historically then Taos has followed a narrow path, both literally and figuratively, which has allowed Taos to survive with a certain mystique and with a preserved sense of antiquity.[6]

Footnotes

1. F.R. Bob Romero and Neil Poese, *A Brief History Of Taos*, (Taos: Kit Carson Historic Museums, 1992), p. 1
2. Corina A. Santistevan and Julia Moore, *Taos A Topical History* (Santa Fe: Museum of New Mexico Press, 2013), p. 51
3. Ibid. p. 53
4. Ibid. p. 55
5. Ibid. p. 54
6. F.R. Bob Romero and Neil Poese, *A Brief History Of Taos*, (Taos: Kit Carson Historic Museums, 1992), p. 26
   Refer to *Taos A Topical History*, p. 54

7

The Pueblo Revolt Of 1680 And Po'pay

El Rebelion De 1680 Y Pope'

Taos historically has long been known as a place of refuge, revolts, and resistance. In fact each major revolt or rebellion that occurred in New Mexico was either planned or hatched in Taos or had a direct connection to Taos as did the Pueblo Revolt of 1680.

For most historians it is well established that the Revolt of 1680 by the Pueblo Indians against the Spanish Colonists occurred because of religious grievances, exploitation and general mistreatment of the Indians by the

Spaniards, and the internal conflicts between the Spanish religious and civil authorities.[1] A leading figure of the Revolt was a medicine man from the San Juan Pueblo (Okay Owingeh) named Po'pay (Pope') who found refuge at Taos Pueblo in 1675 after the San Ildefonso Pueblo Episode in which the Spaniards accused several pueblo medicine men of practicing witchcraft.

Po'pay became active in the Kivas and was then able to quietly and secretly organize the pueblos by preaching the doctrine that all Spaniards should be driven from New Mexico, and the old pueblo way of life restored. Gradually over a five-year time period Po'pay became the center of a wide conspiracy to revolt.[2] Chief among his lieutenants was Luis Tupatu of Picuris Pueblo and other Pueblo leaders. According to Fray Angelico Chavez "a large black mulatto with piercing yellow eyes" named Domingo Naranjo was also very involved with planning of the rebellion from Taos.[3] There is no question that the revolt was carried out with multiple leadership, but Po'pay was the ringleader and the mastermind of the plan. Indian runners carried knotted yucca or rawhide cords as a countdown calendar used to notify every Pueblo of a simultaneous uprising.

Extensive planning, secrecy, and a contingency plan were all part of the ploy in the Revolt of 1680. Word of the Revolt did eventually leak out to the Spanish authorities, nonetheless, and so the Revolt did start early on August 10, 1680. Rising in unison the Pueblo warriors killed more than 400 Spaniards including women and children and 21 Franciscan Priests. In Taos more than seventy Spaniards were killed including two priests. Most mission churches were destroyed and in the process virtually all vestiges of Christianity were eliminated. Over 2,000 Spanish survivors reached the settlement of San Lorenzo near the present day city of El Paso, Texas. The Pueblo Revolt of 1680 was the best planned and most successful, albeit temporary Indian uprising ever to occur on the North American continent.

After the Revolt, Po'pay attempted to govern the different Pueblos that had long maintained a tradition of independent self-governance, and their sovereignty. He failed as a governor to maintain the Native American confederacy that had formed to carry out the Revolt, and some historians claim that he was guilty of abuse of power and even charge that he became a tyrant and a dictator. The legacy of Po'pay was heatedly debated in New Mexico around the turn of the century in the New Mexico State legislature. The debate occurred during the proposal to create a statute of his likeness.[4] Supporters of Po'pay including current leaders and historians of present day pueblos argued that his leadership was instrumental in saving the Pueblo Indian culture from extinction, and therefore he was worthy of the honor in 2005 of being selected as one of only two New Mexicans to be honored with a statute in the National

Statuary Hall in Washington, D.C.[5]

In all probability all people are not going to agree on the different interpretations of history and individuals will have differences of opinion, but all people should understand that everyone in New Mexico and Taos lives under the legacy of various controversial historical figures such as Don Juan de Onate, the Spanish Colonizer of New Mexico, and Po'pay the Preserver of Pueblo Indian culture and both now justifiably have individual statutes at different sites erected in their honor. In 1680 Po'pay took a stand and he changed the course of history.

The Re-conquest of New Mexico for the Spanish Empire was completed by Don Diego de Vargas in Taos in 1696, but there is no question the Pueblo Revolt of 1680 was the most important historical event in New Mexico in the 1600s and these events were a turning point in the history of New Mexico and history of Taos. The era of the Spanish conquistador in New Mexico was definitely over at that time. From this point forward Native American religions were at least tolerated, Native Americans were treated with more respect than before 1680, and Spanish settlers returned to New Mexico with the intent to work the land, develop an agrarian society based on faith, family, and community and they developed the acequia irrigation systems and land grants issued by the Spanish and Mexican governments. In addition, they established multicultural pluralistic communities wherein people learned to respect their differences, and they retained their cultural heritages and integrity that has resulted in new or blended cultural patterns in Taos over time.

Footnotes

1. Calvin A. Roberts and Susan A. Roberts, A History of New Mexico, (Albuquerque: University of New Mexico Press), 1986, pp. 97,100,101
2. Ibid., p. 102
3. Fray Angelico Chavez, My Penitente Land, Reflections on Spanish New Mexico, (Albuquerque: University of New Mexico Press, 1974, p. 182
4. Albuquerque Jouranal, "Battle Brews Over Statute Of Pueblo Revolt Leader" June 12, 1997, p. A1, A8
5. Albuquerque Journal North Edition. "Po'pay Statute Installed In Capitol", September 23, 2005, p. 1-2
   A Statute for Senator Dennis Chavez was installed at the Statuary Museum in Washington D.C. in 1964.

8

Land Grants in Taos Valley

Mercedes En El Valle De Taos

Virtually everyone who lives east of the Rio Grande in the Taos Valley resides on land which is or once was part of a grant of land made by the Spanish or Mexican governments. The legacy of the land grants is that they have had a pervasive and complicating impact on land ownership, land tenure, and land use and water rights ownership and irrigation patterns.[1]

The awarding of land grants was the Spanish and Mexican government idea or way of encouraging citizens to settle and maintain lands in remote New Mexico during the Spanish Colonial Era and the Mexican Period. The Spanish government made land grants of three sorts: to pueblos, to individuals, and to groups of families. The earliest land grant in Taos Valley, was made to the Pueblo Indians of Taos in the 1600s, and is known as the Taos Pueblo League Grant. It was patented by the U.S. government in 1864. Private land grants were made to individuals—usually as rewards for service to the government, especially military service. With continuous occupation, these lands could become the private property of the grantee and could be sold or transferred. The third type, a grant to a group of people, is a community grant. Such a grant awarded individual families a parcel of land that they could farm on and which they could build a house. The bulk of the grant, however, was reserved for shared community use: for grazing stock, for wood gathering and timber harvesting, for hunting and watering, and was not supposed to be sold or transferred to other parties.[2]

Sources of water largely account for the early patterns of settlement in Taos, with grants along the Taos Valley's and the Rio Grande's six tributaries being crucial. Acequias or water irrigation ditches were constructed by the members of the community to irrigate the crops being grown along the narrow river valleys. Throughout the 1700s the resilient Taoseno settlers built ranchos and little villages, called placitas. The New Mexican settlers developed an agrarian communal society that provided for their needs. They treated water and land, especially communal land, as resources for the benefit of the entire community and not just one individual.

Grants of land made by European governments were not unique to Spain. One of the primary conditions in the British colonies, though, was that land was designated as private or public land, whereas in the Spanish colonies such as Nuevo Mexico, community land grants or hybrid land grants with communal land were the norm. This difference became a problem in New Mexico because the land grants were issued under one legal system and adjudicated by another. The result is that much of the land that had been included in the original land grants in Taos Valley, especially the common land, no longer exist as part of the original land grants.

In the long and torturous process to confirm and patent land grant claims during the U.S. territorial period, much precious time was lost, giving unscrupulous speculators and land grant schemers ample opportunity to use devious tactics to acquire land grant lands, usually at the expense of the Spanish-speaking settlers living on the grants. While the surveyor general system was inefficient and incompetent, the Court of Private Claims process was too little too late to protect the common lands of the land grants of New Mexico's Hispano settlers. [3]

There were sixteen patented land grants in Taos County and there are still eight identifiable land grants in the Taos Valley. There were fifteen land grant claims elsewhere in the county that were not confirmed or patented. It is not easy to generalize about land grants, because each of the land grants has its own history and legacy, but it can be said that long established Hispanic communities and the Hispano people suffered an injustice as they lost ancestral common land and private land claims that were part of the original land grants in Taos Valley. The issue of the land grants in Taos remains a contemporary and a contentious topic with continuing efforts by land grant heirs and claimants to resolve disputes and reclaim land.

Footnotes

1. Corina A. Santistevan and Julia Moore,
    (Santa Fe: Museum of New Mexico Press), 2013, p.80
2. Ibid. p. 80
3. Ibid. pp. 83,84

9

The Historic Churches of Taos

Iglesias Historicas De Taos

The Catholic churches of the Taos Valley are not the most common or typical historical landmarks or sites that are usually visited by tourists, but they do possess their own mystique, charm, and special spiritual attraction to Taoseños and to visitors.

Catholicism was introduced into New Mexico by the Third Order of Saint Francis during Spanish colonization and the Franciscan Friars oversaw much of the construction of the mission churches.[1] When the Mexican

Period began in 1821, the Franciscan priests left the area and Padre Antonio Jose Martinez and the fraternity of Hermanos Penitentes are given credit for preserving Catholicism in the area during this period. In 1916 four years after New Mexico statehood had been achieved the U.S. Bureau of Census reported the percentage of religious identifiers in New Mexico at 84.7% Catholic, 11.7% Protestant, and 3.7% other. Currently in Taos there exists a great diversity of over 30 different churches, faiths, and congregations, but the majority of the population of the residents of Taos still remain predominantly Catholic.

The first permanent structure after Spanish occupation that provides solid evidence of a European settlement date is the first San Jeronimo Mission Church at the Taos Pueblo constructed around 1615. The first church, built under the guidance of Fray Francisco Zamora, was destroyed during the Pueblo Revolt of 1680. The second San Jeronimo Mission Church was built in the 1700s

(1706-1726) after the Spanish re-conquest, and destroyed in 1847 when Col. Sterling Price suppressed the revolt, restored order in Taos, and then re-established American authority after the Taos Revolt/Resistance.[2] The existing San Geronimo Mission Church was then built in the 1850s after American sovereignty became official in 1848.

Our Lady of Guadalupe Church in downtown Taos dates to 1801, and began as a mission church of the San Geronimo Parish. Padre Antonio Jose Martinez became the first non-Franciscan priest at the church when he became the priest in 1826. In 1833 Bishop Zuribia of Durango, Mexico decreed that Our Lady of Guadalupe would become a Parish, the first under the patronage of Nuestra Senora de Guadalupe, in present day United States.[3]

The first Lady of Guadalupe Church structure was in service for 109 years before it was deemed as irreparable and a new church was built in 1911. That church structure was destroyed by an accidental fire in 1961. The existing Our Lady of Guadalupe Church was immediately re-built and, was dedicated on December 16, 1962 by Archbishop Edwin Byrne.

The San Francisco de Asis Catholic Church in Ranchos de Taos is commonly referred to as one of the most photographed and most painted churches in New Mexico, and one of the most recognized churches in the United States. The Ranchos Church was completed in 1815 when the alter screen retablos were installed and mass was celebrated. It cannot be stated definitively when actual construction of this widely acclaimed church began because of some confusion and questions about the historical record, but the church was providing Christian services by the summer of 1815.[4] The church was dedicated as a parish by the Archbishop on May 2, 1937, and is now one of only a few historical sites remaining from the Spanish Colonial Period in Taos that is open to the public.

Consequently, since both the San Geronimo Mission Church and the Our Lady of Guadalupe Church are in their third re-incarnation, the San Francisco de Asis Church in Ranchos de Taos is the oldest of these adobe historical Catholic Church structures in Taos. It continues to serve the community as an earthened temple of faith, as an active parish, and a living church that gets renewed life and tender loving care from its parishoners during the yearly re-mudding or "enjare" each spring.

There are a number of other Catholic churches and capillas or chapels in Taos County that serve various communities, but the origins of the three churches featured here all date to the Spanish Colonial Period. These three churches attract tourists for their mystique and for their spiritual ministries as well as for their historical significance.

Footnotes

1. Eleanor B. Adams & Fray Angelico Chavez, The Missions of New Mexico, 1776, (Albuquerque: The University of New Mexico Press), 1956, p. 6
2. Ibid., p. 102
3. The Taos News, A Centennial Celebration Of The Last Great Place, 2012, "A Grand Lady", p. 18
4. Images of Ranchos de Taos church, (Santa Fe: Museum of New Mexico Press, 1988, pp. 117-119

10

Hacienda Martinez

Hacienda De Los Martinez'

The Hacienda Martinez is another important historical landmark in Taos. The Hacienda Martinez is more than 200 years old and events commemorating the bi-centennial celebration of this historic site were held in September 2004.[1]

The Hacienda Martinez had its beginnings when Don Antonio Severino Martinez moved his family from Abiquiu to Taos in the early 1800s and began construction of the Hacienda on a site where a couple of structures already existed. The raids of the Nomadic Indians were still occurring in the Taos Valley and so the Hacienda was constructed in a fortress style for protection.[2]

This was an important time in the Taos Valley even though it was at the tail end of the Spanish Colonial Period. The Don Fernando de Taos Land Grant had been ceded in 1796 and in the process this event along with the establishment of several other land grants had doubled the number of Spanish speaking families in the Taos Valley. Prior to this the Spanish speaking population had been concentrated in the Ranchos de Taos area where the Ranchos Plaza had already been built around 1776.

In the years immediately following the founding of the Hacienda Martinez, Severino Martinez built a flourishing mercantile business trading on the Chihuahua Trail into Mexico, transporting goods from Northern New Mexico, and returning with needed supplies. During this time the renowned Padre Martinez, the oldest son of Severino Martinez, left New Mexico to study for the priesthood in Old Mexico. By 1821 with the onset of Mexican Independence and the opening of the Santa Fe Trail, goods became more available from the United States. Severino Martinez was able to take advantage of this trade from the East by traveling to Las Vegas, NM to buy goods before they reached Santa Fe where a customs tax had to be paid. By 1826 the Hacienda Martinez was at its peak of development and Severino Martinez as an astute entrepeneur and farmer had become wealthy in the operation of the Hacienda De Los Martinez.

Severino Martinez passed away in 1827 one year after Padre Martinez returned to Taos as parish priest at Our Lady of Guadalupe Church. With the death of Severino Martinez the Hacienda passed to his wife and children. Following the death of Maria Del Carmel two years later, the entire estate transferred to the children and their spouses. The youngest son Pascual Bailon Martinez eventually became the sole owner of the Hacienda and he continued to operate the ranch and trade operation until 1882 when he died, and the Hacienda remained with his heirs until 1931.

The Hacienda then had several owners and had fallen into disrepair when it was purchased by Jerome and Anne Milord in 1964. The Hacienda was then purchased by the Taos Historic Museums in 1972. It was restored and has been operated as a living museum since then.[3]

The Hacienda Martinez now hosts thousands of visitors each year honoring the legacy of the old Taos Trade Fair and the contributions of the early Hispano settlers and the French trappers and traders in the Taos Valley. The Hacienda Martinez is also a National Historic Landmark and one of the few Spanish Colonial sites along with the Ranchos Church and the Taos Plaza open to the public.

Footnotes

1. David J. Weber, In The Edge of Empire, The Taos Hacienda of los Martinez, (Santa Fe: Museum of New Mexico Press, 1996, p. 19
2. Skip Keith Miller, La hacienda de los Martinez, A Brief History, p.5
3. Ibid. p. 2

II

Legacy Of Padre Martinez
El Legado De Padre Martinez

P adre Antonio Jose Martinez is perhaps the most prominent historical
figure of Taos, but like other historical
figures such as Po'pay and Kit Carson Padre
Martinez is also an enigmatic and controversial figure in the history of Taos. Padre Martinez can be described quite simply as the parish priest of Taos, or the founder of the first
co-educational school in Taos and New Mexico. He also published the first book and the
first newspaper in Taos as well as all of New
Mexico. However, there is so much more to

relate and to contemplate about this man.

Padre Martinez was born in Abiquiu, New Mexico in January, 1793 to Severino Martinez and Maria del Carmel Santistevan. He grew up at the Hacienda de los Martinez after 1804 when his father moved the family to Taos. Padre Martinez was raised as a young man of privilege and status, but as the eldest son in the family he learned to work hard and to assume large responsibility. He Married Maria de la Luz Martinez in 1812 and fathered one daughter who lived only to the age of twelve.

After the death of his wife he entered the College of Durango Mexico in 1817 and received a liberal education studying Latin, Rhetoric, Canon law, Philosophy, logic and metaphysics. He was ordained as a secular priest in February 1822 and became parish priest in Taos in 1826.[1] He also served as Spiritual Leader and founder of the Moradas and Confraternity of the Hermanos Penitentes and he wrote the regulations for some of the first Moradas that were etablished in Abiquiu and in Taos County beginning in the 1820s. Padre Martinez later guided the Hermanos through the changes that occurred during the Mexican Period and after American occupation and Sovereignty.[2]

Padre Martinez was an educated man of early nineteenth century New Mexico, and he was involved in most of the major events and issues during one of the most interesting and eventful period in the history of Taos. He lived under four sovereigns, if you count the brief time that the Confederate flag flew over Albuquerque and Santa Fe in 1862. He experienced the events of two major revolts, the first in 1837 when New Mexicans rebelled against higher taxes, and the centralized government of Mexico. He was sympathetic to the people that opposed higher taxes, but ultimately he served as military chaplain for the forces under Manuel Armijo that suppressed the revolt and restored Mexican rule to New Mexico.

Padre Martinez fought against the land grant schemers who received high positions in the United States government in New Mexico after American occupation, but he also provided refuge in his home to the surviving families of Governor Charles Bent and Kit Carson after the Taos Revolt/Resistance of 1847. He dealt with the social and political conflicts that were inherent during this time period by routinely assuming the role of conciliator in order to help bring about peace and harmony. He served in the Mexican Legislative Assembly when there was no separation of church and state. He stated that under Spanish and Mexican sovereignty the priests had been allowed to ride the burro, but under American government they would have to be content to walk along behind. So he understood the concept of the separation of church and state and accordingly he changed the emphasis of his school from one that had trained priests to one that trained lawyers.

After American Sovereignty in 1848

he served as President of the first state Constitutional Convention in New Mexico's effort to establish statehood and then worked to establish New Mexico as a United States Territory in 1850. He also served as a member of the New Mexico Territorial Assembly from 1852-1861. He had studied and understood the new American form of government and believed in democracy and he named his Newspaper "El Crespusculo de la Libertad." (Dawn of Liberty).

Padre Martinez's on-going battle with Archbishop Lamy is much debated and some have concluded that he was excommunicated by Lamy. The historical record shows only that he was ecclesiastically censured by Lamy and ultimately he did not continue as a Catholic Priest, but he did continue serving his own church and the communities surrounding Taos and he was not formally excommunicated from the Catholic Church as some believe because Archbishop Lamy did not follow canon law as it is prescribed for excommunication with the Pope and the Vatican as the final authority.[3]

The other major question about Padre Martinez is whether he fathered children outside of marriage and whether he has direct biological descendants. He does have indirect descendants as his many brothers and sisters had large extended families, but the historical record does not prove definitively that he had direct descendants. There are of course families that claim to be direct descendants but Padre Martinez did not claim these individuals as biological relatives in his will or during his lifetime. Thus since the written historical record that includes birth and baptismal certificates is not conclusive, we only have speculation and conjecture and numerous individuals opinions about this question.

In sum, there is no question that Padre Martinez was a very important man in the history of Taos, and very deserving of the statute that is displayed on the Taos Plaza. Like his contemporary Thomas Jefferson he was an advocate for education and a champion of democracy. Like Benjamin Franklin, another founding father, Padre Martinez was a publisher, author, and editor. The accomplishments of Padre Martinez in education religion, government, and publishing are immense and his legacy in Taos and in New Mexico is huge. He was a "man of the people" and a man ahead of his times."

Footnotes

1. Pedro Sanchez, Translation by Guadalupe Baca-Vaughn, Memories Of Jose Antonio Martinez, The Rydal Press, 1978, p. pp.15, 17, 37
2. Corina A. Santistevan and Julia Moore, eds., Taos A Topical History, (Santa Fe: Museum of New Mexico Press), 2013, pp. 252
3. Ibid., p.254, 255 Besides a statue, Padre Martinez is also commemorated with a Hall on the UNM-Taos Campus and a lane in Taos named Padre Martinez Lane.

12

Revolt Of 1837
Rebelion De 1837

The Revolt of 1837 also known as the Chimayo Rebellion was a populist revolt by Native New Mexicans against the Mexican government that was the sovereign government in New Mexico at that time. Taosenos staunchly participated in this defiant uprising over taxes and incompetence and corruption in the Mexican government. In addition to these causes it appears that factional and class politics were also factors in the Revolt.

Manuel Armijo, the Governor of Nuevo

Mexico based in Santa Fe was removed and replaced by Albino Perez in 1835.[1] A complete re-organization of government then occurred in 1836. The office of Alcalde Mayor was abolished and the Departmental Plan, that was implemented by Perez, was very unpopular since Perez was not a native New Mexican. The plan to increase taxes was the last straw for struggling rural New Mexicans. The Indians from the Santo Domingo Pueblo murdered Governor Perez and many of the top officials of his administration. According to historical accounts the episode was so brutal that Governor Perez was decapitated after he was murdered and his head was kicked around like a soccer ball by the insurgents. In the revolt, centered in the Chimayo-Santa-Cruz area, the people met to object to any form of increased taxation. A huge contingent of Pueblo Indians, mixed blood mestizos, and genizaros formed and then marched to Santa Fe. The rebels defeated the 150 man militia of Governor Perez in an ensuing battle and forced the survivors to retreat to Santa Fe.

After the rebels had deposed Perez and his militia, New Mexicans stood at the crossroads of history. They could have followed the path of the United States in 1776 and declared their own independence or they could have followed the example of the Texans wherein one year earlier in 1836 they had declared and won independence from Mexico. However, New Mexico did not follow the path of independence like the United States or Texas probably because the elite leadership in New Mexico did not have a vision for independence. Instead the leadership was divided and they opted to protect the interests of the upper class and to preserve the status quo.

Jose Gonzales, a mixed blood Taoseno, with linage to the Taos Pueblo and the Nomadic tribes, was made interim or defacto Governor of New Mexico. He appointed mostly Indians to most of the governmental posts and expropriated the properties of the former leaders. Manuel Armijo who had been

Governor before Perez, remained loyal to Mexico and he raised a militia to resist Gonzales. Another Taoseno, Pablo Montoya, a former Alcalde of Taos, was the leader of about 3,000 troops who marched on Santa Fe in September only to be defeated by Armijo's forces that were supported by about 300 troops that had arrived from Chihuahua Mexico.[2]

The Mexican Government forces under Armijo met the rebel forces in the final battle in January of 1838 and defeated them, suppressed the revolt, and executed Jose Gonzales.[3] Padre Antonio Jose Martinez of Taos, serving as the Chaplain of the Mexican forces under Armijo, was the confessor for Gonzales. According to one historical account Armijo is quoted as saying "Padre confess this genizaro, hear his confession, so that he may be given five shots." Padre Martinez' role is somewhat of an enigma because by all accounts he would have been sympathetic to the rebels cause as he also opposed higher taxes, but at this point in time he was a member of the elite in New Mexico and he was still loyal to Mexico probably because he had been present in Mexico during the Mexican struggle for independence from Spain and he likely had hopes that Mexico's goals for liberty and democracy would be realized. But more importantly as in most instances he was there to play the role of conciliator and peacemaker.

The down side of the Revolt of 1837 is that because New Mexico did not have the visionary and united leadership like Texas with men such as Stephen Austin and Sam Houston, New Mexico did not follow the path of independence as a sovereign state. Instead Governor Armijo was re-installed as governor and New Mexico continued down the chaotic path of instability and mismanagement under Mexican rule until 1846 when American occupation and then American sovereignty occurred. During the Mexican Period there was so much chaos that 23 changes of government occurred in 25 years. Thus Taos played a part in another revolt with Taoseno Jose Gonzales serving as defacto governor of New Mexico for six months, Taoseno Pablo Montoya serving as military commander, and Padre Martinez serving as military chaplain. The Revolt of 1837 primed New Mexico for the next change in sovereignty that was imminent.

Footnotes

1. Corina A. Santistevan and Julia Moore, eds., Taos A Topical History, (Santa Fe: Museum of New Mexico Press), 2013, p. 118
2. Ibid. p. 118
3. Janet Lecompt, Rebellion in rio Arriba, (Albuquerque: University of new Mexico Press), 1985

13

American Manifest Destiny In Taos

El Destino Manifesto En Taos

I n 1846 Stephen Watts Kearny marched into Nuevo Mexico with the "Army of the West" and occupied New Mexico. United States sovereignty became official two years later when the Treaty of Guadalupe Hidalgo was signed on February 2, 1848 to end the Mexican American War. This event was the culmination of a series of events that began to unfold when the Louisiana Purchase was made in 1803 by the United States. This scenario was a historical prophesy articulated by John O'Sullivan when he wrote that it is the

God given "Manifest Destiny" of the United States to expand from coast to coast.[1]

The Zebulon Pike Expedition in 1806 was a harbinger to what would come to pass when Pike entered Spanish territory on a reconnaissance trip and the significance was that through the publication of his journal in 1810 a lot of the mystery of the Spanish Southwest was removed for Americans. By the early 1800s Spain had become internally weak and was losing control of a once great empire. In 1819 with the signing of the Adams–Onis Treaty the Spanish gave up their claim to Florida and thought they had secured their claim to Spanish possessions west of the Louisiana Territory.[2]

In 1821 Mexico won its independence from Spain and created a political vacuum in Nuevo Mexico and the area that was soon to become the American Southwest. At this point the idea that New Mexico would become part of the United States was inevitable. The opening of the Santa Fe Trail and the activity of the mountain men trappers and traders initiated the economic conquest of New Mexico. The prevailing immigration trends and the change in demographics with people migrating from the east to the west were obvious. Neither Spain nor Mexico had controlled the northern half of Mexico or sufficiently populated the area. These historical forces were undeniable and were in play.

In 1824 Mexico made a grant of land to people moving in to Texas and by 1830 there were over 20,000 immigrants from the eastern United State in Texas. By 1836 Texas won its independence from Mexico and then was annexed by the United States ten years later in 1845.[3] The events in Texas were not necessarily the cause of war but they were an accelerator of the Mexican American War.

The election of James Polk, an expansionist president, in 1844 signaled the events that followed. Polk was unable to get Mexico to sell the northern portion of its county and by 1845 John Fremont with Kit Carson as his guide marched to within 25 miles of Monterrey. On March 8, 1846 American troops under the command of Zachary Taylor occupied a disputed strip of land between the Nueces River and the Rio Grande and then blockaded the Rio Grande.[4] Mexico considered this an act of war and on April 24, 1846 Mexico declared war on the United States and fired on a makeshift American fort near Brownsfield, Texas. On May 12, 1846 the United States after much debate declared war on Mexico and in August of 1846 Colonel Stephen Watts Kearny marched along the Santa Fe Trail with 1700 men, and occupied New Mexico without firing a shot.[5]

The reason there was no immediate resistance from New Mexicans is that there had been so much chaos and instability during the Mexican Period. New Mexicans had even revolted against the Mexican Government in 1837. People like Padre Martinez and Manuel Antonio Chaves, who fought on the side of the Americans, had lost faith in the

Mexican Government and the promise of liberty and democracy, and at this point they were looking to the United States for some hope.[6] The one bit of resistance to "Manifest Destiny", however, would come from Taos in the 1847 Revolt/Resistance.

Footnotes

1. David M. Kennedy et. al, The American Pageant, (Boston: Houghton Mifflin Company), p. 371
2. John M. Blum et. Al., The National Experience, (New York: 1973, pp. 180-181
3. Ibid., p. 262
4. Ibid. p. 267
5. Ibid. p. 271
6. Marc Simmons, The Little Lion of the Southwest, A Life of Manuel Antonio Chaves, (Chicago: The Shallow Press Inc.) p. 102

14

The Taos Revolt/ Resistance Of 1847

El Rebelion/Resistencia De 1847

The Taos Revolt/Resistance of 1847 is an event that happened in Taos on January 19, 1847 about six months after the United States occupation of New Mexico by Stephen Watts Kearny. Even though there are still questions about what happened, the event is probably more accurately described as resistance to American occupation than a revolt. The event is viewed historically as an act against an invasion that had occurred without firing a shot, and the New Mexican insurgents had still not yet been made citizens of the United States.

In the violence that occurred in Taos, the newly appoint American Governor, Charles Bent, was scalped and killed as were other Americans such as Simeon Turley at Turley's Mill near San Cristobal. One question that was debated for years is who perpetuated this violent resistance and why? The answer to the first question has been answered as a loose coalition of Taos Pueblo Indians led by Tomasito Romero and Hispano firebrands from Taos led by Pablo Montoya. The second question of why it happened is much more complicated as it appears that in addition to resistance to American occupation and resentment of the Mountain Man presence in Taos and at Turley's Mill, there was a lot of opposition to the continuing land grant scheming that the new comers were involved in. In addition, the smuggling practices surrounding the Santa Fe Trail trade and the avoidance of paying import duties also planted seeds of discontent and contributed to the intensity of the Revolt/Resistence of 1847.[1]

Regarding the response of the United States military under Colonel Sterling Price the third question that is often asked is why the United States Army attacked the Catholic Church at the Taos Pueblo where the insurgents took refuge when it should have been considered a sanctuary. A good answer to this question has not been forthcoming.

Regarding the aftermath of the Taos Revolt/Resistance and the trials, there is still a prevailing sentiment that there was a miscarriage of justice in the trials of the insurgents because the Judge, Charles Beaubian, was the father of one of the victims, the foreman of the jury, George Bent, was brother to Charles Bent, and one of the insurgents was tried for treason even though he was not a citizen of the United States. Perhaps the most amazing fact, though, is that trials were held at all since, in contrast, to the end of the Revolt of 1837 executions were swiftly conducted with the benefit of a confession, but without the benefit of a trial.[2]

In a nutshell in the aftermath of the Taos Revolt/Resistance of 1847 the United States military officials led by Colonel Sterling Price suppressed the rebellion, and restored order and control of New Mexico.[3] The insurgents or patriots who were fighting to preserve their home land were tried, and then were executed or hung on the Taos Plaza. New Mexico became part of the United States when the Treaty of Guadalupe Hidalgo was signed on February 2, 1848, when the Mexican American War ended. Perhaps for now until more study and research is done by historians and all questions are more satisfactorily answered the most definitive statement that can be made about the Taos Revolt/Resistance of 1847 is that it happened for various reasons. It was not a true revolt nor just a reaction to American occupation and in the end, "frontier justice" prevailed in the aftermath of the Taos Revolt/Resistance and trials of 1847.

Footnotes

1. Corina A. Santistevan and Julia Moore, eds.,
   (Santa Fe: Museum of New Mexico Press), 2013, p. 119
2. Ibid. p. 120
3. Ibid. p. 129

15

Territorial Period In Taos (1850-1912)

El Periodo Territorial Sobre Taos
(1850-1912)

The United States Territorial Period in Taos began in 1850 when the Compromise of 1850 was enacted, not in 1846 when American occupation of New Mexico occurred, nor in 1848 when the Treaty of Guadalupe Hidalgo ended the Mexican American War and established United States sovereignty in New Mexico.

The duration of the Territorial Period was 1850-1912 when statehood was achieved. The Territorial Period was characterized by violence and a lot of turf battles over land

and power. The early Territorial Period in New Mexico included events such as the Civil War battles in New Mexico, range wars between sheep owners and cattlemen, disputes over land grants, and the last of the Nomadic Indian Wars. Taos was affected to some degree by all of these events, but three local seminal events stand out in Taos during the Territorial Period.

One of these events occurred during the Civil War when the Confederate Army invaded New Mexico from Texas. The New Mexico Volunteers under the command of Kit Carson and with a number of Taosenos in military service took part in the Battle of Valverde in Southern New Mexico. Prior to this battle before the start of the Civil War some "Confederate sympathizers" in Taos were tearing down the American Flag on the Taos Plaza.[1] Finally Kit Carson, Ceran St. Vrain, and others took it upon themselves to nail the flag to the flag pole and guard the flag around the clock. Subsequently, Taos began to fly the flag 24 hours a day to commemorate the event and this is the reason that the flag at the Taos Plaza is one of only a few locations in the country that flies the flag both day and night by custom and tradition.[2]

Shortly after the Civil War another significant event occurred in Taos that would have far reaching consequences for the future of Taos. Gold was discovered in the mountains above Taos, and mining played a minor role in the Taos economy for a short period. The Twining mining camp would then become the location where Ernie and Rhoda Blake started the development of Taos Ski Valley in 1956. However, the "white gold" of Taos Ski Valley would have a much greater long term economic impact than the sparse gold and copper that was mined in Twining in the 1870s. In addition, the Taos Ski Valley has greatly impacted Taos as the catalyst in the transition toward a resort recreational based community.[3]

Another pivotal event in Taos during

the Territorial Period is known as the "Broken Wheel Episode" that led to the establishment of Taos as an art colony. American artists were drawn into the Taos Valley in the late 1800s in part because Taos had remained relatively isolated as a result of being missed by the Santa Fe Trail and the railroads. This influx of newcomers in Taos was made up of artists such as Ernest Blumenschein and Bert Phillips who arrived in 1898. Their arrival was in part accidental. They were on a sketching trip to Mexico from Colorado, when a wheel broke on their lightweight surrey in the vicinity of San Cristobal. Blumenschein then carried the wheel on his horse to Taos to get it repaired. When he saw Taos, Ernest Blumenschein knew immediately that he had found his new home. Other artists followed and they gradually established the Taos Society of Artists in 1915, and as a result Taos developed as a world renowned art colony in the twentieth century with it mixture of natural beauty, mountain light, culture, and tradition.

With the turn of the century a cash economy began to take hold in Taos and within 50 years tourism, art, and recreation became the economic base for Taos. The decline of the barter economy and the crush of consumerism and materialism affected the simpler life of Taos. Subsistence agriculture which had sustained Taosenos for centuries did not keep pace with economic appetites and by the middle of the 1900s subsistence farming was no longer a viable way to support a family. Taos which for so long had resisted change began to see dramatic change at the end of the Territorial Period.

Footnotes

1. "U.S. Flag Flies Day and Night at Taos". (1967, January 15), Denver Post-Roundup
2. Blanch C. Grant, When Old Trails Were New, The Story of Taos, (Glorieta: The Rio Grande Press, Inc.) 1983, p. 163
3. F.R. Bob Romero and Neil Poese, A Brief History of Taos, (Taos: Kit Carson Historic Museums), 1992, p. 23
4. Ibid. p. 23

16

The Legacy Of Kit Carson

El Legado De Kit Carson

The legacy of Kit Carson as a historical figure is an enigma as he is viewed as both a hero and a villain depending on the community and perspective. Christopher "Kit" Carson was the most famous of the mountain men in Taos, even though he was not the first mountain man nor the one with the longest tenure in Taos.

Kit Carson arrived in Taos from Kentucky, through Missouri on the Santa Fe Trail in 1826. He was a contemporary of Padre Martinez until their deaths one year apart, Padre

Martinez in 1867 and then Carson in 1868. As a mountain man he travelled throughout the Rocky Mountain West and lived outside of Taos more than in Taos. During this time he had two Indian wives, and had one child that was raised by his family in Kentucky. With the decline of the fur trade the mountain men lost their economic viability and by the 1840s the mountain men turned to other pursuits. Kit Carson settled in Taos for a while and married Josefa Jaramillo and together they had eight children. He achieved fame in the 1840s as John C. Fremont's guide to California and as such is regarded as a frontier scout and a link in the connection of the continent from coast to coast. He also guided Colonel Stephen Watts Kearney to California after the conquest of New Mexico in 1846.[1]

In addition, Kit Carson also served as an Indian Agent in the 1850s, and as a military officer in the Civil War in 1862. He was involved in the pacification and seduction of the nomadic Indian tribes in the last of the Indian Wars in New Mexico. He helped to subdue the Navajos in 1864 and the Mescalero Apaches in 1863. He also fought against the Comanche's in late 1864 and has been accused of using forced removal to reservations and scorched earth tactics by destroying fields, gardens and fruit trees that caused women and children to starve.[2]

So what is the legacy of Kit Carson? From the Native American perspective he is certainly not a hero, but from the Anglo American perspective he "led the way" and helped open the West for American settlement and expansion. Kit Carson House and Museum, Kit Carson Park and Road, Kit Carson Electric Coop, Carson Army Base, and Carson National Forest, and a number of towns and municipalities in the West commemorate his legacy. He was a man of his times and his reputation as an Indian fighter was unfairly sensationalized by the dime novels.[3]

Similar to other New Mexico historical figures such as Juan de Onate and Po'pay we should judge Kit Carson in the context of history and the circumstances of the time. We all should understand that the animosities of the past were sometimes unavoidable consequences of different societies and cultures that came into contact and so conflicts and confrontations did occur. And no ethnic group can claim that their ancestors were never guilty of atrocities against another group.[4] The focus now in hindsight should be forgiveness and the healing of the wounds and scars of the past and the coming together of different people. Taos today with its historical diversity can become a model for implementing cultural pluralism in the region, the country, and the world, the turbulent history of the area notwithstanding. Under the concept of cultural pluralism, diverse people respect their differences and retain their cultural heritage and integrity, and learn how to live together in harmony and peace.

Footnotes

1. Marc Simmons, *Kit Carson & His Three Wives*, (Albuquerque: University of New Mexico Press), 2003, p. IX
2. Ibid. p. IX
3. Marc Simmons and R.C. Gordon McCutchan, *The Short Truth About Kit Carson and the Indians*. (Taos: Kit Carson Historic Museums), 1993, p. 6-7
4. Ibid. p. 8

17

Historic Diversity Of Taos

La Diversidad Historica De Taos

When we think of how best to describe Taos the words that come to mind most often are diverse or the historic diversity of Taos. Over the centuries a number of different kinds of people have come to visit and to live in Taos. This was true long before the term tri-cultural Taos was being used. The fact is that multi-cultural Taos or cultural pluralism in Taos are much more appropriate terms to use to describe Taos.

Historically, even the people of Taos

Pueblo were diverse, as they descended primarily from the early Anasazi, but over the years have had a lot of customs and influences injected from the nomadic tribes (dress, food, and dances etc.), principally the plains Indians. One legend about the Taos Pueblo is that two groups arrived at about the same time at the site of the Pueblo and both groups built their homes on either side of the Rio Pueblo. Regardless of whether this is legend or fact, over the past 400 years different Native American groups and individuals including Comanches, Apaches, Navajos, and genizaros have settled in Taos. Genizaro is a term used to describe full-blooded Native Americans that became detribalized and then learned Spanish, embraced Christianity and accepted and acculturated into Hispanic villages.[2]

The Spanish Conquistadors that came to New Mexico were also the product of a mixture of many diverse groups that settled on the Iberian Peninsula between 2500 B.C.

and 1492 A.D. The mixture of people that included Celts, Iberians, Greeks, Romans, Germans, Jews, and Muslim Moors evolved into one of the most diverse melting pots found anywhere in the world. The blending of people continued in the New World everywhere that the Spanish settled, as the Spanish mixed with African slaves and Native Americans and their descendants became part of the group we now know as Hispanic or Latino. In this process of amalgamation, the terms Mestizos and Mulattos were added to the mix.

In Taos the term Spanish became the popular label under which most people were labeled and later classified by both the U.S. Census and the State of New Mexico, regardless of ethnicity. The Spanish label grew to include the influx of the French from the Louisiana Territory and mountain men and fur trappers of all ethnic backgrounds that came into Taos in the late 1700s and early 1800s.[3]

The influences of the Anglo Americans, which is also a broad inclusive term, were added to the Taos mosaic during the American occupation, and this wave of people has had its own diversity that included traders, artists, merchants, bohemians, intellectuals, hippies, new agers, and retirees.

The Mexican influence that is attributed to Mexican Independence in 1821 continues today with the influx of Mexican immigrants that strengthens the resilience of the Spanish language, arts, music, foods, and cultural holidays such as Cinco de Mayo.

Historically, Taos is a mecca that has attracted a multitude of diverse people and somehow, Taos has found energy, strength and vitality in all its dynamic waves of influences and diversity. This is cultural pluralism, and diversity alive and well in Taos.[4]

Footnotes

1. Corina A. Santistevan and Julia Moore, Taos A Topical History, (Santa Fe: Museum of New Mexico Press), 2013, p. 65
2. Fray Angelico Chavez, My Penitente Land, Reflections on Spanish New Mexico, (Albuquerque: University Of New Mexico Press), 1966, p. 200-202
3. Corina A. Santistevan and Julia Moore, Taos A Topical History, (Santa Fe: Museum of New Mexico Press), 2012, p 15
4. F.R. Bob Romero and Neil Poese, A Brief History Of Taos, (Taos: Kit Carson Museums), 1992, p 25

18

Taos In The 20th Century

Taos En El Siglo Viente

The 1900s were a time of significant changes in Taos with the arrival of the artists and other colorful characters.[1] At the beginning of the 1900s Taosenos began to see the introduction of a cash economy and by mid-century, the barter and agricultural based economy of Taos, or in other words, the butter and egg economy was replaced by the tourism and recreational based economy.[2]

Early in the 20th century, the artists and Avant Garde intellectuals, and other colorful characters that came to Taos included

Bert Phillips and Ernest Blumenschein, Joseph Sharp, E.I. Couse, Oscar Berninghaus, Walter Ufer, Buck Denton, Mable Dodge Luhan, Georgia O'keefe, Photographers Ansel Adams and Paul Strand, Psycho analyst Carl Jung, Arthur Manby, Nicoloi & Eva Fechin, Victor Huggins, D.H. Lawrence, Frieda Lawrence, Dorthy Brett, Doc Martin, John Collier, Burt & Elizabeth Harwood, and Millicent Rogers. All of these individuals and others left some kind of legacy in Taos that includes existing museums, books, art pieces, the founding of an art colony and the beginning of a community health facility that became Holy Cross Hospital.[3]

At the same time that the new arrivals were coming into Taos some native born Taosenos were leaving. First During WWI when Taos soldiers served in large numbers overseas. Then during the 1930s, 1940s, and 1950s Taosenos left in mass exodus due to the effects of the Great Depression, WWII, and in the 1950s due to new post-war economic opportunities in California, Utah, Colorado, and other states. The census of 1940 and 1950 were the only two in the 20th century that the population in Taos County showed a decrease from the previous decade.[4]

The influence of the Hermanos Penitentes and the Moradas also decreased significantly in Taos during this time since at least one male member of most families were members of a Morada in the early 1900s, but this was no longer the case after the end of WWII when Hermanos that returned after having served their county and having seen other parts of the world in many cases no longer lived in Taos nor continued to be active in the Moradas.

Other important events in Taos during the last century include the achievement of statehood which meant the introduction of a new layer of government in Taos. Then in 1934 the Town of Taos was incorporated as the first municipality in Taos County. The incorporation of the Town of Taos happened as a result of the horrific fires that occurred in the early 1930s on the Taos Plaza. The dire need for fire protection was recognized and as a result a Town was formed in order to establish a fire department.

In 1956 the Taos Ski Valley was started by Ernie & Rhoda Blake and this milestone injected the economy of Taos with a new emphasis on recreation. The catalyst for the construction of the Rio Grande Gorge Bridge was George Lavender, owner of Pot Creek Logging. He wanted to bid on timber on the other side of the gorge and when he became chairman of the highway commission in New Mexico he secured funding to build paved roads on U.S. Road 64 up to both sides of the Rio Grande gorge without a commitment for the State to build the bridge. For a few years this road was called "The Road To No Where". The Taos Gorge Bridge was completed in 1965 and it opened Taos up to the West and the North as access to and from southern Colorado and other parts of Taos County became easier.[5]

The "Hippie Invasion" of the late 1960s

and early 1970s was in a sense a continuation of the influx of an eccentric element that Taos had seen as early as the visits of the diverse participants of the Taos Trade Fair in the 1700s and the arrival of the Mountain Men in the early 1800s, and the artists and Avant Garde intellectuals in the early 1900s. The Hippies were attracted to Taos because they felt that Taos due to its communal self-subsistence agrarian history was the ideal place to work the land and build a utopia. Communes such as New Buffalo and Morning Star were built but were short-lived. But some of the inhabitants stayed in Taos or have returned and have now blended into Taos and still form the nucleus of a New Age Community in Taos.

During the 1970s, 1980s, 1990s and the first decade of the 21st century Taos County has had significant growth in population , and a change in demographics has occurred. More retirees and more people that see Taos as a place to have a second home have arrived. Also the majority of the children of native-born Taosenos have been leaving Taos for employment and educational pursuits elsewhere. But since at least fifty years is needed for a clear perspective of the window of history, it is difficult to conjecture what this will mean for Taos in the 21st century. The increase in population between 1970 and 2010 that almost doubled in Taos County from 17,516 to more than 33,000, is due to in-migration, but will probably not continue at the same levels because the population of the United States is leveling off and the population of the world is now declining.[6] But Taos is still a multicultural community that is in transition in other ways. Community development in Taos can mean that Taos could become a model wherein diversity is valued. New technologies could be developed in business, education, communications (internet), and energy (solar and wind), all could provide better jobs, and community resources such as water should be used wisely and be sustained for future generations.

Footnotes

1. F.R. Bob Romero and Neil Poese, A Brief History of Taos, (Taos: Kit Carson Historic Museums), 1992, p. 23
2. Ibid. p. 25
3. Ibid. p. 24 Mable Dodge Lujan was instrumental in the establishment of the convent that eventually became the Holy Cross Hospital.
4. Town of Taos, Vision 2020 Master Plan, Mayor Fred Peralta
   and Town of Taos council, Adopted February 1999,. P. 26
5. The Taos News, September 1-7, 2011, My Turn, "Why Don't They Bridge It?", John Himes, p. A7
6. George Friedman, The Next 100 Years,A Forcast for the 21st Century, (New York: Random Books), 2009, p.52-59

19

Taos Fiestas
Fiestas De Taos

L as Fiestas de Taos, more formally known as *Las Fiestas de Santiago y Santana* are not a commemoration of a specific historical event in Taos. The Fiestas de Taos are currently an Hispanic event held on either the 3rd or 4th weekend in July. The annual summer cultural celebration has evolved over time. It has both secular and religious underpinnings, but can best be described as a socio-economic community celebration of cultural pride.

Historically, fiestas in general can be

traced to various community functions that revolved around the Catholic Church. Each small community or village had it respective church or capilla that had it own Patron Saint such as Los Cordovas Capilla that celebrated *El Dia de San Isidro* on May 15th, or Our Lady of Guadalupe in Taos that celebrated on December 12th. Each small community's day was different and the celebration was a distinctive fiesta or function for each community or village.

The history of the current Fiestas de Taos began in the 1930s by people that had recently arrived in the Taos community and were active in the emerging arts community. The main objective of the Taos Fiestas at that time was a marketing ploy to boost the tourism economy and the arts in Taos. The founders of the Taos Fiestas, though, gave the Fiestas religious overtones by inviting the community and the Catholic Church to sponsor a Fiesta Queen Pageant. Then they named the Fiestas for Santiago, Patron Saint of Spain, and Santa Ana, the Grandmother of Jesus.

The Fiestas de Taos were to a degree also modeled on the Espanola Fiestas and the Fiestas de Santa Fe which do commemorate specific historic events of the Spanish Conquistadors. The Espanola Fiestas celebrate the colonization of Nuevo Mexico by Don Juan de Onate in July 1598, and the Fiestas de Santa Fe honor Don Diego de Vargas and the beginning of the Spanish Re-conquest of Nuevo Mexico in 1692. Some efforts were made early on to make the Taos Fiestas coincide with a historical event. In 1940 Las Fiestas de Taos were recognized as the "Cuarto Centennial fiestas" and were named the Coronado Fiestas to acknowledge the Taos visit of Hernando de Alvarado in 1540. In recent Taos Fiestas *Caballeros de Alvarado* have participated in the fiestas parade, but the 1540 historical event as the main focus of the Taos Fiestas has never quite become the accepted viewpoint.

By the 1950s the Fiestas de Taos was

still a cross-cultural extravaganza, but by the 1960s the organizers and proponents of the Fiestas became predominantly Taos Hispanics and the non-Hispanic participants that had included people from the Taos Pueblo declined significantly. Other national and state events of that decade contributed to this. The Chicano Movement was in full swing and *El Movimiento Chicano* emphasized Hispano pride, assertiveness, and political activism. Some factions of the Chicano Movement such as the Alianza Movement led by Reis Lopez Tijerina advocated radical and violent tactics to reclaim land grants in New Mexico. Then the "Hippie Invasion" of the late 1960s alarmed all Taosenos, regardless of ethnicity, and the large number of hippies present in Taos in 1968 actually caused the Fiestas de Taos to be cancelled for that year.

By the 1970s the Taos Fiestas event emerged as a pre-dominantly Hispanic community celebration and in the 1980s this reality was formalized with the creation of a Taos Fiesta Council made up of predominantly Hispanic leaders.

The current celebration is still primarily a Hispanic attended event with the non-Hispanic elements of the community not as active as they were back in the 1930s, 1940s, and 1950s. But the non-Hispanics members of the community are starting to become more involved, especially with the Tio Vivo ride, an attraction that is owned and sponsored by the Taos Lions Club. In addition, recently there has been some participation by the Gay Community in the fiesta parade and the Azteca Dancers have appeared on the entertainment schedule on the Taos Plaza. This recent activity and participation by the broader community harkens back to the beginnings of the Taos Fiestas and the event could morph one more time to become a truly comprehensive and inclusive community celebration of Taos community pride.

Footnotes

1. Corina A. Santitevan and Julia Moore, eds., Taos A Topical History, (Santa Fe: Museum of New Mexico Press, Publishers), 2013, p. 81 The patron saints of other Taos Churches include San Francisco de Asis in Ranchos de Taos and Nuestra Senora de Dolores in Canon.

2. Dr. Sylvia Rodriguez, Retired Professor of Anthropology, University of New Mexico in lecture made to the Taos County Historical Society, June 7, 2014.

3. Ibid.

4. F.R. Bob Romero, Adjunct Instructor, University of New Mexico-Taos, These are observations that have been made by Romero, the author, as a participant and celebrant of the Taos Fiestas since 1960s and the father of Ana Alicia Romero de Gonzales, Taos Fiesta Queen in 2007.

5. Ibid.

20

History of Water Uses, Acequias, Water Rights And Agriculture In Taos

Historia De Las Aguas, Acequias, Derechos De Agua, Y La Agricultura En Taos

S in *Agua No Hay Vida* "Without Water There Is No Life". This slogan has been heard and has been true in Taos since time immemorial. This is the reason the Taos Pueblo was built on either side of the Rio Pueblo, and why the sources of water from the six rivers determined the patterns of the land grants, acequias, and population settlement in the Valley.

The history of water uses before American occupation and the history of water rights after American sovereignty have undergone

151

periodical changes. Prior to American occupation water uses in Taos were principally for agriculture and the necessary domestic uses. Native Americans depended on water for irrigation of their crops and Hispano settlers developed the acequia system in the process of developing an agrarian based subsistence economy and an agrarian society that endured until the mid-1900s. Long and short term droughts have been common throughout the known history. Generally cooperation and sharing was the rule in the use of the water during times of drought.

When American sovereignty became a reality in 1848, though, water rights also became an issue. The Hispanic and Native American view of the ownership of water could be summed up in this saying, "As long as the waters flow and the grass shall grow, the pastures and water shall be held in common." The Anglo American perspective was more in line with the idea that whoever owns the land owns the water which is in concert with the concept of riparian water rights, that is more common in the eastern states. Thus from the time of American occupation through the Territorial Period, water came to be seen more as a commodity that could be bought and sold than a precious community resource to be shared.

When the Treaty of Guadalupe Hidalgo was ratified in 1848, water rights as a personal property were guaranteed. In 1850 after New Mexico became a United States Territory, through the Compromise of 1850, the Territorial Legislature enacted water laws protecting the acequias as basic units of government. In 1891 the Court of Private Claims confirmed water rights that existed before American sovereignty, and the New Mexico Territorial Legislature re-affirmed this in 1907. When New Mexico achieved statehood in 1912 the Doctrine of Prior Appropriation was embedded in New Mexico Constitution and this doctrine basically states that whoever can prove that they made beneficial use of the water first has the better water rights.

Adjudication is a legal process to formally and finally establish priority dates and ownership of water rights in a particular area, watershed, or stream system. Although some water rights within New Mexico have been fully adjudicated the process is still not complete in the Taos Valley. A lawsuit known as the Abeyta Case that was initiated in the 1960s involving ownership of water in the Taos Valley has not been fully resolved. When the case is completed, the legal process will determine who in fact has legal ownership of some of the water rights in the Taos Valley. More importantly if or when the water rights are then transferred or sold and severed from an irrigated property, those water rights fully becomes a commodity and can more readily be sold on the open market.

In summary, due to the on-going adjudication process, the uses of water and the ownership of water rights are in the process of changing once again. Native American Tribal governments will seek to retain as much of their water rights and traditional uses as possible. Acequias will attempt to retain as many of the water rights intended for irrigation and agriculture within the acequia system, and municipalities and developers and domestic water associations and water and sanitation districts will seek to purchase and transfer water rights to develop water systems that serve the growing needs of an increasing number of households in the Taos Valley.

Footnotes

1. This slogan is popular in general in Taos and is the slogan of El Valle de los Ranchos Water and Sanitation District.
2. Acequia Timeline, Taos Valley Acequia Association, 1998
3. Ibid.
4. Constitution of the State of New Mexico, Mary Herrera, Secretary of State, October, 2007, p. 165
5. A Short Introduction to New Mexico Water Law, John Draper, Lecture at Water Conference in Santa Fe, September 10, 2012, p. 5

21

Christmas In Taos

La Navidad En Taos

The History and story of Taos is not complete without an essay on Christmas in Taos. Historically the Catholic Christmas traditions are the oldest Christian traditions in the area and they blend in perfectly with the more contemporary American Christmas traditions such as the Lighting of LeDoux and the lighting of the Christmas tree on the Taos Plaza on the first week in December.

The Catholic Christmas traditions in Taos begin with the masses celebrating

Advent around the first part of December. Advent observes the beginning of the time period when Christians begin to prepare for the arrival of Christ the Savior. On December 12th the observance of the appearance of the Virgin de Guadalupe is celebrated in Taos. The celebration of La Virgin de Guadalupe is particularly popular in Taos because Nuestra Senora de Guadalupe is the Patron Saint of the Catholic Church in downtown Taos, the first so designated (1833) in the United States.[1] The story of the apparition of the Virgin de Guadalupe to Juan Diego, an Indian peasant, is important to Hispanic Catholics in the United States and to people in Latin America because the event in 1531 on the hill of Tepeyac near Mexico City was the catalyst that symbolizes the acceptance of Christianity by indigenous people of the Americas. San Juan Diego was canonized in 2002 by Pope John Paul, and the Virgin de Guadalupe continues to be an important religious symbol for Hispanic Catholics in Taos.

The celebration of the Christmas season in Taos continues in earnest on the 16th of December with the onset of the celebration of the Posadas, complete with abuelos, farolitos, and luminarias. The Posadas are celebrated for nine nights and culminate with the Posadas mass on Christmas Eve. The Posadas are a re-enactment of Mary and Joseph seeking shelter before the birth of Christ or essentially they depict the first Christmas and thus signify the true meaning of Christmas. The participants in the dramatization are initially denied entrance or shelter at the Inn, but either on successive nights of after persistent efforts are allowed to enter the home or church where the Posadas are being held and the celebrants then enjoy songs, prayers, and refreshments such as biscochitos, empanaditas, chicos, and posole.[2]

The Christian Christmas tradition is also observed at the Taos Pueblo with the dramatic Christmas Eve procession and the Christmas Day Matachines Dance or Deer

Dance. The holiday festivities in Ranchos de Taos continue with the mid-night mass or Misa del Gallo, and the Christmas day masses are celebrated throughout the valley and Taos County. In Ranchos de Taos the Christmas festivities are extended to New Years Day with the appearance of the Los Comanches who claim to be descendants of Native American people (Genizaros) that accepted Catholicism. The Comanches visit the various homes that have a Manuel or Manuelita residing or visiting and they dance in honor of the arrival of the Savior Emmanuel.[3]

In addition to these traditional activities, Christmas is particularly special in Taos because all of the American society traditions of Santa Claus, Christmas trees, decorations, and exchange of presents have been embraced in Taos in tandem with the traditions of holding Matanzas and the baking of treats such as empanaditas and biscochitos that have also been retained.[4] The continuation of Christmas holiday plays such as Los Moros Y Los Cristanos and Los Patores are other examples of Christmas traditions still common in Taos.

The Hispanic Catholic and Native American holiday celebrations, though, have become a curiosity and anomaly because of their uniqueness and continued vitality. People are attracted because of the depth of roots and tradition and the continuity of spiritual life that these Christmas traditions represent. In essence most Taosenos seem to have a special affinity with Christmas in Taos and Christmas outside of Taos is just not the same for them. In addition, all aspects of the traditional Christmas are warmly embraced and celebrated in Taos, making the holiday a true cross-cultural experience.

Footnotes

1. Taos: A Celebration Of The Last Great Place, 2012
   Complimentary Edition of the Taos News, p. 18
   The original Lady of Guadalupe Church was built in 1801
   by the Franciscans, and was decreed as Nuestra Senora
   de Guadalupe in 1833 by Bishop Zubiria of Durango,
   Mexico.
2. It is interesting to note that Hanukkah, the Jewish
   celebration of "the festival of lights" occurs close to
   December 16th.
3. F.R. Bob Romero and Neil Poese, A Brief History Of Taos,
   (Taos: Kit Carson Historical Museums, 1992), p. 8
4. A Matanza is the tradition of butchering livestock like
   hogs, sheep, or cattle before the holidays so that there
   would be plenty of meat for cooking. One tradition
   known as "Pidiendo mis Crismas" that was a tradition
   similar to Halloween where children would take their
   sacks around the neighborhood asking for "Mis Crimas"
   or "My treats" is no longer practiced in Taos.

22

History Of Government In Taos

Historia Del Gobierno En Taos

The governing of Taos has historically been challenging and problematic because Taoseños tend to be vigilant and are prone to rebellion on occasion. The history of government in Taos can be traced for about 1,000 years since about the time of the kiva clans and subsequently the people of Taos Pueblo were practicing their own unique blended form of governance and spirituality before the arrival of the Europeans.[1]

When Spain colonized the area in the 16th century Spanish Colonial Administration was imposed, although quite often it was only on the surface. The Spanish Colonial form of government was very rigid, legalistic, and centralized, and the influence of the Franciscan missionaries almost made the Spanish form of government a theocracy. However, since Taos was isolated as the northernmost outpost during the Spanish Colonial Period, there was almost no sense of identification with a state or nation. The people of Taos developed a distinct independence of character and were able to implement self-governance similar to the thirteen colonies in the East, and thus maintained a spirit of individualism and vigilance.[2] Nonetheless, many Spanish government institutions such as the land grants, the missions, the plazas, and the acequias were super-imposed upon the people of Taos. The acequias are the oldest form of written government in New Mexico and in fact all of North America. Under American sovereignty the acequias are operating and active entities and have continued to the present as a basic unit of local government.[3]

After Spanish sovereignty ended in Taos in 1821, the transition to Mexican rule was fairly passive. The sitting governor did not even leave office immediately, but gradually major changes did occur. Partidos as geographic divisions of government were implemented and would become roughly the same geographic units that would become counties during the U.S. Territorial Period in 1852. Under the Partido system an Alcalde Mayor was the chief governmental officer with judicial functions, powers in law enforcement and administration. In 1836 a re-organization took place and this led to the Revolt of 1837. Jose Gonzales from Ranchos de Taos was named the governor of Nuevo Mexico for six months and then was eventually captured and promptly executed by Manual Armijo. Mexican rule was then restored.[4]

Ten years later there would then be a Taos Revolt/Resistance to American occupation that was centered in Taos, when newly appointed Governor Bent was murdered. The resistance was quickly suppressed by Col. Sterling Price in January 1847. The Taos insurgents were put on trial and hung on the Taos Plaza and in a miscarriage of justice one was even convicted of treason even though Taosenos were not yet American citizens.

Government in Taos under United States Sovereignty has been noted for the introduction of a democratic form of government with separation of church and state, and based on a constitution that provides for civil liberties and civil rights. Voting rights have been realized incrementally by various groups such as Hispanics, African Americans, Women, and finally Native Americans in 1948.

The first true courthouse, a Territorial Style adobe and wood structure, was built under American sovereignty in 1880 on a site on the Taos Plaza where a "jail and a crude courthouse" had existed since 1830 during the Mexican Period. In the 1930s the courthouse that had been built in 1880 was destroyed by fire. In 1934 the new court house that is now the old historic courthouse on the plaza was completed and the Taos County government moved in. A new modern courthouse was then built and occupied on the current site on Paseo del Pueblo Sur in 1970 and was used for 38 years. The new existing complex on Paseo del Pueblo Sur was built in 2008-2009, and currently serves as the Taos County Judicial and Administrative Center.[5]

From 1846 to 1848 New Mexico and Taos were governed under the Kearny Code, although in 1847 after the Taos Revolt/ Resistance Taos was for all practical purposes governed under martial law. In 1848 U.S. Sovereignty became official under the provisions of the Treaty of Guadalupe Hidalgo. From 1850 until statehood New Mexico was governed as a United States Territory, and since 1912 Taos has been governed as a county within the State of New Mexico. The Town of Taos was incorporated in 1934 and a total of four incorporated municipalities now exist in Taos County, which include the Village of Questa, Town of Red River, and the Village of Taos Ski Valley.

Governing in Taos remains challenging. The politics and the elections of Taos remain contentious and passionate. The political squabbles, debates, disputes, and confrontations that take place, however, are all visible signs of a vigilant and vibrant democracy in action in Taos.[6]

Footnotes

1. Taos: A Celebration Of The Last Great Place, 2012, Complimentary Edition of the Taos News, Taos Politics Has A Long,Turbulent History, p.54
2. F.R, Bob Romero and Neil Poese, A Brief History Of Taos, (Taos: Kit Carson Historic Museums, 1992, p. 8
3. Asequia timeline, Taos Valley Asequia Association, 1998
4. Janet Lecompt, Rebellion In Rio Arriba, 1837, (Albuquerque: University of New Mexico Press, 1985.
5. Old Taos County Courthouse-timeline, David Henry, Architect, p. 1-2
6. Taos: A Celebration of the Last Great Place, 2012, complimentary Edition of the Taos News, Taos Politics Has A Long Turbulent History, p. 56

23

History Of Education
In Taos

Historia De La Educacion En Taos

E ducation has always been important but also difficult and challenging in Taos. Before the Europeans arrived the Indians of the Pueblo de Taos lived their lives according to a religious belief system and corresponding ritual that had to be learned and embraced. This was a form of education. In order to get a "clear and concise picture of the development of the history of education" in Taos it is important to give credit to the role played by the early natives of Taos.[1]

When the Spaniards arrived in the 16th century the main objective of the Franciscan missionaries was to convert the Indians to the Christian faith and to teach the Spanish language in the mission schools. No serious efforts to successfully establish formal education for the common people were made during the Spanish Colonial Period, and any instruction that occurred at that time was left entirely to the Catholic Church.[2]

During the Mexican Period (1821-1846) "Padre Antonio Jose Martinez played an important part in the educational development of the County of Taos." "Between 1826-1856 he was engaged in educating young people of both sexes in reading, writing, and arithmetic."[3] The efforts of Padre Martinez gives credence to the claim that Taos is "the cradle of New Mexico's formal education", since his school was the first in New Mexico even before American Sovereignty.[4]

Even though a few parochial schools, such as the Alice Hyson School and other

Protestant mission schools, were founded during the Territorial Period (1850-1912) it was not until the New Mexico Territorial Legislative session of 1891 that a comprehensive public school system was inaugurated in New Mexico. It was under this law that the educational system of the 20th century in Taos County was organized. In 1912 when New Mexico achieved statehood, the State Department of Education was created and the Superintendent of Education became an elective office in each county.[5] One-room adobe school houses were the norm at that time and they were hampered by chronic issues of inadequate school supplies, questionable teaching methodology, and inadequate financing of the schools.

In the early 1960s the current public school system with separate school districts within the county, a superintendent, and an elected school board managing the school district was established in Taos County. This system with minor adjustments such as inclusion of charter schools that operate under the auspices of the Taos School District is still in place. There has been a pervasive emphasis on standardized testing that was mandated by the state and federal government. In addition public schools still suffer from overcrowding in the classroom and not enough teachers and inadequate supplies and facilities.

Higher education had its origins in Taos in the 1970s when a broad selection of classes were offered through New Mexico Highlands University (NMHU) and Northern New Mexico College/University to meet the demand of returning Viet Nam veterans that had G.I. Bill educational benefits. Some smattering of college courses had been offered before in previous decades. These diverse course offerings in the 1970s were formalized in 1982 with the establishment of the Taos Educational Center that operated under the Off-Campus Instruction Act.[6] Both NMHU and Northern served as parent-institutions, and during this time Taosenos were poignantly advised by State officials that Taos would not be allowed to build a permanent college campus and instruction of college classes would have to take place in existing public school facilities.[7]

In 1993 University of New Mexico was selected by the local school board as parent-institution, and worked in concert with the off-campus advisory board, which was the locally elected school board. Construction of first phase of Klauer Campus began with a $1.6 million appropriation that had been made in 1990 by the state legislature. This effort was spearheaded by a dedicated group of Taos activists and community citizens that bucked the conventional wisdom, secured the donation of land from the Klauer family, and saw their efforts to build a permanent college campus in Taos come to fruition.[8]

The University of New Mexico had a long presence and history in Taos prior to 1993 as the owner of the Harwood

Foundation Museum since the 1930s and the D.H. Lawrence Ranch in San Cristobal. In 2003 UNM-Taos became a branch campus through the efforts of administrators and legislators. The UNM-Taos community college campus continues to expand and to serve the growing higher education needs of the Taos community.

In sum, the history of education for both public schools and higher education has faced many challenges and obstacles through the years. However, Taosenos have shown great resilience and determination in supporting improvements and in spearheading progressive reforms in the educational institutions of Taos. After some 200 years since Padre Martinez' first school opened it can be stated that education in Taos is alive and well, particularly in higher education, and it has not been strangled in the cradle.

Footnotes

1. Enos Garcia, Education in Taos County, Masters Thesis, p. 27

2. Ibid. p. 29

3. Ibid. p. 30-31

4. Ibid. p. 33

5. Ibid. p. 40

6. The Taos news, Your Turn, "Take Advantage of College Courses Here, August 9, 1984. Bob Romero Editorial, p. A-6. Bob Romero served as Director of the Taos Educational Center from 1984-1993 under Highlands and Northern and served on Taos Municipal School Board and Off-Campus Advisory Board from 1993-1997. Some courses, primarily in archeology have also been offered through Southern Methodist University since the 1970s at their Pot Creek Campus.

7. The Taos News, "Chances Slim To Start Community College", Judy Romero, December 1984

8. The Taos News, "UNM Takeover of Education Center Begins" June 3, 1993, p. A-3

24

The Seven Wonders of Taos

Los Siete Milagros Y Maravillas De Taos

T aos is a very inspiring and attractive place and some have even said it is mystical or possessed of magic and wonder. Clearly there is a mysterious and supernatural quality to Taos that is intriguing. Some people after moving to Taos have been asked why they have come to Taos, and they have responded saying something to the effect that "I felt I was called to be here." For all the above reasons it is appropriate and essential to attempt to identify the Seven Wonders or Miracles of Taos.[1]

The number one attraction on the list of the Seven Wonders of Taos is without question the Taos Pueblo. One of the chapters in the book (Chapter 5) is entirely devoted to The Taos Pueblo and that information is accessible. Suffice it to say here that the Taos Pueblo is still the most visited tourist attraction, and the prime reason is that the Taos Pueblo represents longevity, humility, spirituality, resiliency and tenacity.

The Rio Grande Gorge Bridge site on Highway Road 64 is number two on the list of the Seven Wonders of Taos. The gorge is even older that the Taos Pueblo and the gorge bridge site is probably the second most visited tourist attraction in the Taos area. More information on this site is available in Chapter 4 and 18 of this book. The Rio Grande Gorge Bridge has gained some notoriety as it has become a place where some have chosen to end their life. Authorities have not determined how to best deal with this morbid attraction of the bridge, but for a big majority of people the attraction of the Rio Grande Gorge Bridge continues to be a positive and enlightening experience.

The third Wonder of Taos is the Sacred Taos Mountain and the adjacent Taos Ski Valley (TSV) situated on the north face of the mountain. The Taos Mountain and the TSV resort are part of the southern chain of the Rocky Mountains named the "Sangre de Cristos" by the Spaniards. Many residents believe in the spirit of the Taos Mountain to safeguard Taos[2], and some also believe that the mountain will either embrace you or reject you as a Taoseno. The Taos Mountain is also known as "Pueblo Peak" for some and it is called Ma Who Lo or Ma-Ha-Lu in the language of the inhabitants of the Taos Pueblo.[3] This scenic area around the TSV easily qualifies as one of the Seven Wonders of Taos for the natural beauty, the recreational opportunities, and its mysticism and its local lore.

The fourth Wonder of Taos is the Taos plaza which some refer to as "El Corazon de Taos" or "the Heart of Taos." Traditionally in Hispano culture a plaza is a town square where people gather for commerce, and religious, cultural, and civic functions. The Taos Plaza has served this role for over 200 years. If the walls of the Taos Plaza could tell tales they would range from conversations between Kit Carson and Padre Martinez in the 1830s to encounters among mountain men, American merchants, Anglo artists, and 1960s hippies. Even more intriguing would be to hear what actually happened in the early morning of January 19, 1847 when Governor Charles Bent arrived back in Taos and encountered a mob made up of Hispano Taosenos and men from the Taos Pueblo.

Some of the contemporary highlights and significant features of the Taos Plaza are the Old Taos Courthouse which houses the New Deal murals, the statute of Padre Martinez, the Chinese Wall, Ledoux Street named for a mountain man and that leads to the Harwood Museum of Art, the Juan

Largo St. named for Long John Dunn, the Kit Carson House and the Governor Bent House on Bent Street. Over the years the Taos Plaza has evolved from a community square that witnessed many different kinds of historic events to an accidental theme park where visitors flock to see and attempt to sample a bit of Taos and locals congregate on special occasions such as the Fiestas de Taos.

The fifth Wonder of Taos is the San Francisco de Asis Church in Ranchos de Taos Plaza. The Ranchos Plaza is older than the Taos Plaza and was built in the 1700s for protection against the nomadic Indians threat. The 200 year old church, completed in 1815, is the oldest existing Catholic Church structure in the Taos Valley. This "earthened temple of faith" is unique because even though it is an active church, it is also a tourist attraction. It is recognized as a National Historic Landmark and it houses the famous mystery painting by artist Henri Ault. The Ranchos Church is also different because it is one of the few churches in the country that is still maintained in an old traditional way by parishioners and volunteers that congregate for the yearly mudding or "Enjare" during the first two weeks in June.

The sixth Wonder of Taos, the Hacienda Martinez, is another Spanish Colonial site open to the public. It is also featured in a chapter 10 of this book, and it currently hosts thousands of visitors yearly and honors the contributions of early Hispanic settlers in the Taos Valley, and the participants in the Taos Trade Fair of the early 1800s. It is a historic site that should not be missed by anyone with an interest in the history of Taos.

The seventh Wonder of Taos is not a physical structure or natural feature, but is instead an abstract or intangible idea that is left up to the imagination of the reader. The seventh Wonder of Taos could be the diversity of Taos, since Taos is probably one of the most diverse small communities in the United States. It could be the ever present creativity of Taos that is personified by the Taos artists of so many different stripes. The seventh wonder of Taos could be the spirituality of Taos that is evident in the ancient native religious rites of the Native Americans, the historic influences of Catholicism, and the presence of other religious beliefs and belief systems, such as in the New Age community of Taos. Other aspects of the intangible wonders of Taos are the para-normal phenomena such as the Taos Hum, the legendary Tunnels of Taos, the prevalent lore of aledged U.F.O. sightings, and stories of ghosts, witches and haunted houses. All of these intangibles draw people to Taos and give Taos a certain mystique of awe and wonder.

Footnotes

1. This is an observation of the author serving in various capacities for 30 years plus.
2. F.R. Bob Romero and Neil Poese, A Brief History of Taos, (Taos: Kit Carson Historic Museums), 1992, p. 25
3. Corina A. Santistevan and Julia Moore, eds., Taos A Topical History, (Santa Fe: Museum of New Mexico Press, Publisher), 2013, p. 10

25

400 Year Celebration Of The History Of Taos-2015

El Cuarto Centenario Sobre La Historia De Taos-2015

I n the year 2015 the Taos community cel-ebrated 400 years of history as a European settlement. Taos is arguably the fourth oldest occupied European settlement within the present boundaries of the United States. In addition several other historic events in Taos were celebrated in 2015 as multiple cen-tennial anniversaries. The entire community has showcased the history of Taos and the unity of the various cultural, religious, and ethnic communities within Taos.

As stated earlier in addition to the

Native American indigenous founding, Taos also has a distinctive and relevant European founding. The name of Taos as it is known today is first found in the historical documents that relate to the *Don Juan de Onate* Colonization of New Mexico in 1598. The European founding date of Taos, though, is attributed to 1615 when Taos Pueblo was declared a village by the Spanish government and the first San Jeronimo Mission Church, the first European structure in the Taos Valley, was being constructed. Some Spanish Settlers began to live in Taos at this time. These are the events of 400 years ago that were commemorated in 2015.

Another milestone event 300 years ago was also celebrated in 2015. This event occurred after the Pueblo Revolt of 1680 followed by the Re-conquest of New Mexico by Don Diego de Vargas that was completed in 1696. By 1715 the reissuance and occupation of the Cristobal de la Serna land Grant and the granting of the Gijosa Land Grant constituted the resettlement and re-establishment of Spanish civil government in Taos Valley. This constitutes three centuries of land grant and acequia history in the Taos Valley.

The Ranchos de Taos area was settled before the area of Taos proper as a result of this occupation and settlement of the Serna Land Grant, and by 1796 the Spanish speaking population in the Taos valley numbered around 300 residents that lived mostly on the Serna Land Grant in Ranchos, and this population doubled in 20 years.[1] By 1815 according to the historical documentation the San Francisco de Asis Church was completed.[2] It is not completely clear, however, when construction of the Ranchos Church began. As one priest at the Ranchos Church stated, "The Church is 200 years old, but it took us 100 years to build it." In any case the completion of the church with its unique alter screen was in use in 1815 and this is then a bicentennial commemoration that was being extensively celebrated by the parish and the community of Ranchos de Taos in 2015.[3]

The year 1898 marks the "Broken Wheel Episode" that brought the two artists with the names of Bert Phillips and Ernest Blumenschein into Taos. The event foreshadowed the activities of 1915 when the Taos Society of Artists was founded and this then began the process that led to Taos becoming a world-renowned artist colony. The 100 year anniversary of this event is also part of the celebration that was commemorated in 2015 by the Taos Arts Community.

Consequently, there were at least four important historical events in Taos that occurred 400, 300, 200, and 100 years ago that were worthy of celebration in 2015. The founding or discovery of Taos by Europeans 400 years ago is at the forefront of the celebration. The year 1715 when Spanish civil government in Taos Valley was re-established is especially important to the Hispanic community. The completion of the Ranchos Church in 1815 is a noteworthy celebration for the community of Ranchos de Taos, and the 1915 founding of the Taos Society of Artists is a milestone for the Taos Arts Community. All of these notable historical events include the entire multi-cultural community of Taos. Perhaps the grand celebration of 2015 will truly bring together the diverse elements of the Taos community, and all can celebrate the history and unity of Taos.

Footnotes

1.   Corina A. Santistevan and Julia Moore, eds., Taos A Topical History, (Santa Fe: Museum of New Mexico Press), 2013, p. 86

2.   Images of Ranchos de Taos Church, (Santa Fe: Museum of New Mexico Press), 1988, pp. 117-119

3.   The Arroyo Hondo Land Grant was also ceded in 1815 and was one of three land grants granted in the Taos Valley between 1796 and 1815 that substantially increased the Spanish speaking population in the Taos Valley.

¡Yo soy Taoseño!

F. R. BOB ROMERO

Yo soy de Taos, un valle Viejo, en el norte de Nuevo México. Taos es un lugar muy mentado y tambien muy visitado. Nadie sabe definitivamente el origen, del nombre y el significado es un misterio. Algunos dicen que Taos no es lugar ni espacio. Pero en realidad es un estado de la mente y del cerebro. Y un gran poder al centro del universo. Entre los Taoseños hay mucho tipo de diversidad. Y todos tienen sus puntos de vista, y sus propios cuentos de la verdad.

¡Yo soy Taoseño!

Yo soy el indio de Taos, orgulloso, noble y espiritual. Yo he vivido aquí desde el tiempo inmemorial. Y todavía, de espíritu y la mente, yo sigo siendo fuerte e independiente. Por muchos siglos y siglos, yo he luchado contra fuerzas extranjeras, y yo he preservado.

¡Yo soy Taoseño!

Yo soy nativo del Pueblo de Taos, un monumento memorial, y envuelto en mi fe y mi espíritu natural. Yo continúo sembrando verduras, maíz, y hablando Tiwa. Y balanceando la vida moderna, con mi cultura tradicional.

¡Yo soy Taoseño!

Yo soy el Comanche, un descendiente de los indios nómadas. Montado a caballo, en el tiempo pasado, yo pasé por este valle recogiendo lo que ya era mío. Y volando como el viento que corre, para preservar la línea de mis antepasados y mi modo libre. Y luego aquí en Llano Quemado, poblé y me mezcle.

¡Yo soy Taoseño!

Yo soy el conquistador Hispano de España, quien hice el viaje para este paraíso más de cuatrocientos años pasados. Yo vine aquí buscando oro y plata, y desparramando mis semillas y proclamando mi Santa Fe. Yo regresé después de la gran Rebelión, y la Reconquista. Para regar con las aguas, trabajar la tierra y criar el ganado que sostenía, mi familia y la economía.

¡Yo soy Taoseño!

Yo soy el Genízaro con sangre de indio. En una época pasada, como un criado, yo fuí adoptado. Y en veces yo fuí vendido y comprado. Pero yo acepté la hispanidad y la religión cristiana, y Jesucristo como mi salvador sobre la vida eterna. Por muchos años yo he entendido profundamente que yo soy Español, solamente en nombre. Y yo he aprendido que en los ojos de Dios, todos somos iguales como hijos y como hermanos.

¡Yo soy Taoseño!

Yo soy el hombre montañero, vestido de cuero, quien viné con mis trampas, persiguiendo el castor, el aguardiente, y las Taoseñas más hermosas. En esa era pasada yo vivía en las montañas como los indios. Y cuando me fui, yo despedí mis raíces y los apellidos francéses y mi vida gloriosa de los espíritus libres.

¡Yo soy Taoseño!

Yo soy el Mexicano quien en el año 1821, gané la independencia como la República de México. En seguida mi patria resultó libre, con constitución nueva y democrática. Pero el norte, la tierra de Aztlán, fue pérdida en la guerra. Y mi pariente, el Chicano ahora es ciudadano allí. Por mi parte, el país sigue sin fronteras, y yo todavía estoy aquí.

¡Yo soy Taoseño!

Yo soy el Americano de los Estados Unidos. Yo vine correteando el destino manifiesto y buscando nuestra oportunidad. En el año 1848, a mi me tocó ser el soberano. Yo traje la democracia, una forma de gobierno con la esperanza de la justicia y el deseo de la igualdad. Yo introduje la economía libre, y los mercados abiertos. Con el deseo de la competición, y la promesa de la prosperidad.

¡Yo soy Taoseño!

Yo soy el coyote, como mi primo en México. Nosotros somos cuates de la vida, con sangre y parentela de dos lados, pero aceptado completamente en ni una. Yo existo en el desierto en mi vida proscrita. Pero con una perseverancia fiereza, llena de esperanza.

¡Yo soy Taoseño!

Yo soy el artista y el bohemio, pobre y rico. En este lugar viejo, yo soy un reciénvenido. Yo traje mi talento y mi capacidad de crear, para documentar y también preservar la paradoja de este valle y para darle nacimiento, a otro paradigma para un mundo nuevo.

¡Yo soy Taoseño!

Yo soy el nativo y paisano de Taos, de cualesquier linaje. No importa mi color, mi nacionalidad, mi credo, mi lenguaje. Yo tuve la buena suerte de haber nacido en este paraíso, y de cultura, de fe, de familia y de comunidad, yo soy rico. En verdad yo soy del mundo y yo soy de la raza cósmica. Y nadie me negará mis raíces o mi herencia.

¡Yo soy Taoseño!

Yo también soy el extranjero porque yo no soy nacido o criado aquí. Yo fuí llamado como visitante, al paraíso, pero todavía no sé si el paraíso me quiera o me abrazará a mí. Yo vine con el bien sentido de querer vivir aquí. Y en tiempo yo también sabré, si el monte sagrado me aceptará a mí.

¡Yo soy Taoseño!

Y ahora, yo miro a toda la diversidad, en un barco histórico. Somos Indios, Hispanos, Mexicanos, Americanos, Nativos y extranjeros, o cualesquier otro nombre que otros me han puesto o sólo me he puesto yo. También somos vivos, curiosos, religiosos, mañosos y hermosos. Nosotros tenemos la sabiduría que todos podemos sobrevivir si estamos unidos. Pero si estamos apartados y divididos, yo sólo me ahogaré. Si Dios quiera todos viviremos eternamente, y yo perduraré.

¡Yo soy Taoseño!